The Sequence of English Medieval Art

by the same author

★

ARTISTS OF THE WINCHESTER BIBLE

Plate 1

THE CHRIST OF PITY
THE THREE MARYS AT THE SEPULCHRE
THE APPEARANCE TO MARY IN THE GARDEN
THE MEAL ON THE WAY TO EMMAUS

From the Psalter of Robert de Lisle. East Anglian XIVth Century, end of first quarter. See p. 48

THE SEQUENCE OF
ENGLISH MEDIEVAL ART

illustrated chiefly from

Illuminated MSS, 650-1450

by

WALTER OAKESHOTT

FABER AND FABER LIMITED

24 Russell Square

London

First published in mcml
by Faber and Faber Limited
24 Russell Square London W.C.1
Printed in Great Britain by
R. MacLehose and Company Limited
The University Press Glasgow
All rights reserved

OPVS HOC QVALECVNQVE
C.W.D.P. ET M.J.R.
DEDICAT AVCTOR
AMICVS AMICO · MAGISTRO DISCIPVLVS

Preface

This book has been planned as a general survey of English medieval painting. Though so much medieval full-scale painting in England is now in a condition in which only the expert can discern something like the original in what remains, the decorated manuscripts make it possible to extend an illustrated survey right back to Anglo-Saxon times, and while some other material has been used, I have relied chiefly on the manuscripts throughout. The artistic achievement thus revealed is unsurpassed, over the period taken as a whole, in Western Europe. And in spite of two notable books by Dr. E. G. Millar, which—as anyone familiar with them will see—have provided much of the basis for my own, many people are still unaware of this achievement.

My plan involved an immediate problem as to what books could rightly be described, in the earliest part of the period, as English. Was the style, of which the masterpiece is the *Lindisfarne Gospels,* developed in England or in Ireland? This has been one of the most widely debated questions in the history of art. I was fortunate in that the discovery of the Sutton Hoo treasure, with its magnificent jewellery belonging to the crucial period, and the publication of the first four volumes of Professor E. A. Lowe's *Codices Latini Antiquiores,* making readily accessible a mass of comparative data for the books of the time, had transformed the problem, and perhaps brought something like a final solution within sight. As the question has caused such controversy, it seemed desirable to give in detail the arguments justifying my selection of these early 'English' books. They are elaborated in Appendix A.

To collect these plates in the post-war world has not been easy, and I have to thank not only many librarians but many friends also whom I have bothered during the last five years with requests for help: Mr. A. J. Collins and Mr. Francis Wormald in the Manuscript Department of the British Museum, and Mr. T. D. Kendrick and Mr. Bruce Mitford in the Department of Medieval Antiquities; Dr. R. W. Hunt at Oxford; Mr. J. P. T. Bury and Sir Ellis Minns at Cambridge, M. Porcher in the Bibliothèque Nationale in Paris, the authorities of the United States Military Government in Germany, and the

First Secretary of the United States Embassy in London who made possible my approach to them; officials in the Library of Trinity College, Dublin, and in the Public Library in New York; Mr. Charles Mitchell for help in securing photographs from Rome; Canon Shirley at Canterbury: Canon Harrison, Chancellor and Librarian of York Minster; Canon Wallis, Librarian of Lichfield Cathedral; and the Librarian of the Courtauld Institute in London, that admirable organisation to which so many students concerned with the history of art owe so much. For permission to reproduce photographs I am indebted to the Trustees of the British Museum, the Director of the Victoria and Albert Museum, to Bodley's Librarian at Oxford, to the authorities of Trinity College, Dublin, of the Bibliothèque Nationale, of the Vatican, and of the Public Libraries in New York and Stockholm; to the Deans and Chapters of Canterbury, York, Winchester, and Lichfield; to the Masters and Fellows of Pembroke College, Cambridge, and of Corpus Christi College, Cambridge; to the Provost and Fellows of Eton and the Warden and Fellows of Winchester; to His Grace the Duke of Devonshire, to the Bishop of Chichester, to Mr. Herbert Read, and to Mr. C. W. Dyson Perrins. I cannot enumerate those whose works I have found invaluable, but it is perhaps not invidious to name Dr. E. G. Millar, to whose book on the *Lindisfarne Gospels* (in addition to those already mentioned) I have constantly referred, Mr. T. D. Kendrick, and Professor E. W. Tristram. If Miss Joan Evans' great book on *Medieval France,* in which she relates changes in artistic production to changes in demand, had appeared before my own was in proof, I should have been tempted to develop the scattered remarks in this book on the same theme. Sir Sydney Cockerell— most incisive of critics—has taught me many lessons; but it would take genius, not simply learning, to rival his connoisseurship. I am deeply grateful to two distinguished scholars, Mr. T. D. Kendrick and Professor R. A. B. Mynors, who have been kind enough to read proofs and to help me to eliminate mistakes. My book is dedicated to two men to whom I owe debts of a special character; Mr. C. W. Dyson Perrins, who has allowed me the privilege of handling his wonderful manuscripts again and again, and Dr. M. J. Rendall, from whom, though I was never formally his pupil, I have learnt so much about the history and appreciation of art.

Finally a word of gratitude must be added to my publishers and the technicians working for them. Colour reproductions can seldom be wholly satisfactory. They have allowed me to send back plates repeatedly in the attempt to improve them, and to reject plates for which the blocks had already been made, because we could not secure an adequate result from them.

WINCHESTER COLLEGE, *August 1949*   WALTER OAKESHOTT

Contents

I

The Medieval Artist and His Theme

The illustrations which are the main feature of this book were chosen to show the most important changes in the work of artists working in England during the eight hundred years from A.D. 650-1450. Before these changes are discussed, however, it may be well to say something of the ground which all these men have in common. For the Northumbrian artists of the period before Charlemagne, the Winchester artists of the time of Stephen or Henry II, and the East Anglian artists of the later thirteenth and early fourteenth centuries share certain attitudes which differentiate their work notably from the art of the Renaissance or later periods. Thus they have no interest in a naturalistic representation of their subject, or in furnishing a naturalistic setting for it. If they draw a tree or a beast or a fish, they do so either because it is an essential part of their pattern; or because it is part of the story— as the lion is essential to the story of David rescuing the lamb from the lion's *Pl. 26* jaws; or because it is a symbol, like the lion of St. Mark or the eagle of St. John. *Pls. 2, 15b* The artist painting after 1450 was normally concerned to make his work convincing as a naturalistic picture, and his landscapes were often crowded with incident having no essential relationship to his subject. It was a part of his job to show that subject in a setting of ordinary, everyday life. He might draw Icarus *Note i* falling from heaven, but the ploughman would be working in the fields. Business as usual. It might be St. Jerome working in that study, but the study *Note ii* would be such as any more ordinary student of the scriptures would be delighted to possess. And if tradition presented a problem by insisting that Jerome should have a lion with him—a relic of the medieval symbolism that will be discussed later—this would be made plausible and ordinary by representing it like a large, but delightful, and obviously entirely tame, tabby cat. This representation of every subject as part of normal existence is typical of Renaissance painters, who were out of sympathy with medieval themes like the Ascension or Last Judgment. It is as if they had to make their religious pictures convincingly realistic if they were to persuade anyone to believe in them. But the medieval artist was under no necessity of making his pictures convincing, for no one then

B [1] O.M.P.

Pl. 50

needed convincing that David rescuing the lamb, or St. John standing at the foot of the Cross, or the Archangel Michael slaying the dragon, or the Four Horsemen of the Apocalypse, were as real as anything else with which he was concerned. And so when one of our artists sets his figures against a landscape, it is a sure sign that the Renaissance has already begun.

Pl. 15a
Pl. 53a
Pl. 17

The medieval artist, moreover, is almost invariably working with a series of symbols, all of which are clues to refer the spectator precisely, or at least beyond all reasonable doubt, to the subject that he is representing. Some of these symbols are purely conventional or traditional. The symbols of St. Mark and St. John have been mentioned already. St. Luke's symbol is a heifer, St. Matthew's an angel, and these four symbols are part of the ordinary vocabulary of every medieval artist. And so when the Anglo-Saxon artist of the *Grimbald Gospels,* draws a figure 'nimbed' (with a halo) to show that he is a saint, and with a desk, pen and book to show that he is a writer, the symbol of an Evangelist is added to particularize still further, and the subject being then precisely defined, the pattern may then be elaborated as the artist wishes. And if he chooses,

Pl. 15a

like the artist of the *Lindisfarne Gospels,* to add the Saint's name, that is not because the name is necessary, but because it can be used as part of the pattern. He may then go on to say more that occurs to him about the Evangelist. The artist of the *Lindisfarne Gospels* was evidently illustrating a tradition of the fourth Gospel as the work of the 'disciple whom Jesus loved' rather than the possible alternative of the writer completing his work in extreme old age. He is concerned therefore with the Evangelist's youth and devotion, with the youthful disciple who has lost his Lord. The artist of the *Grimbald Gospels* set himself to illustrate the Evangelist's divine inspiration. And these additions may of course be intensely vital. The less realistic a creature is, the more alive it may

Pls. 12, 13, 14

be, like the animals in the *Lindisfarne* or *St. Chad Gospels,* whose round eyes seem positively to gleam with life. But the artist working in such a convention will probably be satisfied if his drawing expresses a single mood or a single quality, dignity, horror, tenderness, or whatever it may be. The complexity of a whole character is beyond his scope. A single characteristic is within it.

Pl. 22

A famous Anglo-Saxon *Last Judgment* may be taken as an example of these principles. On the left is a queue of nimbed figures, evidently saints, and of martyrs, indicated by the palms they are holding, marshalled by the Archangel who is checking their names in the Book of Life. Standing apart from the main queue, though clearly interested in its destination (for he too is seeking admission to the heavenly city) is the Abbot of the New Minster, at Winchester, there because the book comes from that monastery and was written during his period as abbot. It does not matter what clothes the Abbot will in fact be wearing when the Last Judgment occurs. The artist gives him his ecclesiastical

[2]

vestments to show his rank, and so that there may be no mistaking, puts his name, Aelfgar, against him. On the opposite page the Judgment is already in progress. The heavenly city is symbolized by its massive protecting walls. Within it there is no need of a temple or church, such as is so often shown in medieval representations of a city, for the Lord God is himself its surpassing glory. Into it leads a door, with the proportions of which, in comparison with the walls, the artist has not the slightest concern. All that matters is that he should make its purpose clear. It is being opened by St. Peter, here as elsewhere indicated by the immense keys that he carries; and he beckons the elect to enter. In the middle tier of the drawing there is in progress a vigorous fight between the heavenly powers, represented by the Archangel, again with his book containing his list of the elect, and a devil (whose make-up has unmistakable signs of wickedness about it) for a soul, symbolized here as often by the figure of a child. The soul's name is written in the Book of Life. It is clear that he will be rescued. The devil is already having much the worse of the encounter. But a different fate awaits others. What that fate is, is shown in the lowest tier of the drawing, where Hell's mouth, symbolized by the mouth of a giant whale-like monster, with the teeth, nostril and eye prominently shown—the details are significant of the destructiveness of hell and its power to seek out its victims—gapes open to receive them, while devils ram them down to their doom. Here is the story, told by the artist with few details, but with all the detail that is necessary. The artist has used it in the first place to make the most delicate and dainty outline design with touches of colour, secondly to express his astonishing gift for indicating mood by a few deft touches. The firmness of the Archangel marshalling the queue, the expansive politeness of Peter at the door, the thoroughgoing determination of the Archangel's blow and the obvious discomfort that it causes, the lovely pathos in the rescue and the doom of the souls, the dignified but unmistakable interest of the Abbot in his own future destiny, are all indicated with masterly economy. And because we are concerned with a series of human emotions, the artist has reduced his representation of God to a very small size so that the insuperable problem of achieving, on this scale, the contrast between the divine majesty and human frailty is avoided. It was a contrast which later medieval artists who had the great scale of a stained glass window or a wall surface with which to work, often represented.

Many of these medieval pictures have a charm which speaks for itself. But they were intended to be 'read' as well as enjoyed. When David is shown, he is not simply an excuse for the artist to represent youth. The details of the story of David are always in the forefront of the artist's mind, and he may have in mind also the further symbolism of supposed analogies between Old and New Testament scenes, David rescuing the lamb from the lion being taken as prefiguring the *Pl. 26* casting out of a devil by Christ, his rescuing of a lamb from the bear the

Pl. 16 'Harrowing of Hell'. If we cannot understand the language, if we cannot see in the single hand that reaches down into the design the hand of God reaching from heaven with a message for humanity, we shall miss half of the artist's intention. He is reminding us, not of nature in general, but of an actual event, and if we are fully to appreciate his work, some comprehension of the symbols he uses is an essential prerequisite.

Phases of Medieval History

So far we have been discussing matters that are hardly controversial, matters of grammar and vocabulary. When we begin to divide the medieval period up into different phases, and especially when we discuss the relationship of artistic changes with these different phases, there may be occasion for wide disagreements. The game of relating art history to political or social history is dangerously attractive. For it has no rules, except plausibility, and thus frequently involves a large disregard of fact. Artistic tendencies are a law to themselves, and one of the fine arts may often appear to be out of relation, at a given time, with the rest of them, as well as with social or political history. We might argue from the solid appearance of an Anglo-Saxon church or the thick and clumsily turned balusters in an Anglo-Saxon arched window that the artistic mentality of the Anglo-Saxon was solid and bucolic—till we find the Anglo-Saxon draughtsman producing work of an ethereal delicacy. The Norman conquest might be expected to be accompanied by an obvious break in the history of the arts in England, and indeed the work of the Norman architects shows a notable series of innovations. But the manuscripts, as Mr. Wormald has demonstrated, show no such break, and some of the artists who worked in the early twelfth century appear as the direct successors of those who worked in the early eleventh. Sometimes a technical innovation is the cause of a minor artistic revolution. The discovery of a method of laying leaf gold on a prepared surface instead of painting gold onto the vellum in the form of powder suspended in some gummy or oily liquid, brought about an important change in the later twelfth century artist's idea of what an illumination should be. Social and economic changes may show themselves, not merely in the accidents like the style of dress portrayed but in the essentials of works of art. As the market for illuminated Books of Hours extended in the later middle ages to the merchants and bourgeoisie, and as book production became increasingly commercialized in response to this, quality and inspiration tended to decline. But it is a paradox that whereas this may be true of England at that period, the work of the best Flemish and Dutch illuminators remains exquisitely fine. To find the reasons for this difference might take the

Pls. 18, 20, 21

enquirer far into the intricacies of economic history, or it might lead him in some quite different direction. Accordingly any judgments formed about the reasons for the changing phases in this sequence of painting must be put forward with reserve. The phases themselves may be obvious. The reasons for the changes are anybody's guess. The guesses made in the following paragraphs suggest connexion between the history of painting and many different aspects of history, and perhaps one of the few safe generalizations that can be made is that a wide variety of influences must be taken into account.

The first point brought out by this series of plates is that in spite of some common factors to which attention has already been drawn, we are not here concerned with an art that is static. There may be some value in distinguishing at once two main phases within the eight centuries which form our period. The transition from one to the other is marked by the revival of learning. This revival is often confused with the Renaissance and put in the fifteenth and sixteenth centuries. But it begins far earlier, and is already immensely significant by the twelfth, while the centuries from the twelfth to the fifteenth are *par excellence* a period of learning, a period of too much learning perhaps—a period when the works of those 'doctors', the fathers of the Church, the writers of Rome, the Arab scientists, and, through them, the Greeks who were responsible for much of their inspiration, were studied with insatiable thoroughness and their views accepted with unquestioning confidence. It was at this time that Universities began to be founded in Western Europe. In the twelfth century the work of Euclid and some of the work of Aristotle became generally available in translation in Western Europe. The main ideas of classical astronomy began again to be widely current. The books of the great Greek physicians began to be studied. What did not happen however, except in a few rare instances, was independent investigation of any scientific or political problem, or independent criticism of the tradition which was being thus recovered. Accordingly the later medieval period is an age of learning and systematization, the Renaissance an age of observation, experiment and criticism. And for us with our period ending on the eve of the Renaissance, the significant line of division is between what we might call in this context an age of innocence and an age of learning, a line which may be drawn about the year 1100. And in terms of these plates, the division will come between Plates 22 and 23, and shows itself in the severity and self-consciousness, for example, of Plate 24 as compared with the brilliant sketchiness of Plate 22. Socially also the division is important. On one side of it lies, in Western Europe, a society that is predominantly rural, on the other a civilization that speedily becomes urban. For urbanization, and the growth of urban democracies, is one of the main features of later medieval times. With the Renaissance was to come, especially in England, if not indeed a general movement 'back to the land', at least a movement of the main industry (the textile industry) from towns to the country, and a growing fashion on the part of the man who made his money in the cities, to invest it in property in the country. But that lies outside our period, which ends in the hey-day of the mayors, the city corporations and the city guilds. We shall not go far wrong if we reckon that most of the illustrated books produced in England or in Flanders in the fifteenth century were the work of urban craftsmen working on paid commissions. The first such master whose name we know was William de Brailes, in the thirteenth century, who has been shown by Mr. Graham Pollard to have worked in Oxford. This commercial production of decorated books in the later medieval period is a topic to which we shall return later.

Within these two main phases it will be convenient for us to distinguish five. The first, often called Hiberno-Saxon, but here called the Northumbrian phase, lasts from 650 to 850, and is followed by a break of a hundred years or more. The second, from 970 to 1100, is that in which the so-called Winchester School flourished. This period is here called the Late Anglo-Saxon. The third, extending through the twelfth century and roughly limited to it, is called the Romanesque, the fourth from 1200 to 1340 the Early Gothic, and the fifth, from 1340 to 1450, the Late Gothic. Dates given are of course approximate and it is to be noted that in medieval times the transition between one style and another probably often took longer than changes in style in more recent times; so that a painting done thirty years on the wrong side of one of the lines drawn, may nevertheless belong to the style which according to our dating has not yet begun or is already over.

III

The Northumbrian Period 650-850

As the name 'Hiberno-Saxon' often given to it implies, the art of the first period to which Plates 2 and 9-15 in this book belong, has often been assumed to be Irish in origin. This assumption has been vitiated by recent discoveries, particularly by the find of Saxon jewellery from the mid-seventh century at Sutton Hoo, almost contemporary with the earliest books here illustrated, and showing many important artistic similarities with them. It is indeed almost certain that the most famous book of this phase, the *Book of Kells*, was produced in Ireland. But it is equally certain that others are English and that the essential elements in the style (except perhaps for the drawing of the human figure) are not Irish, but Anglo-Saxon. As the style seems to spring almost out of nothing—for there are no books with decoration that is in any way comparable produced in the centuries preceding the making of the *Book of Durrow* in England, or in Ireland, or on the continent, it is worth while to consider the conditions under which it came into being, and the particular stimulus which made Northumbria the centre of its production.

Pls. 2, 9, 15

To explain such an art if we imagine England to have been at that time a place only of brutality and savagery would be impossible. The Saxon invasions had created chaos in England in the fifth and early sixth centuries. But after the arrival of Augustine's mission in 597, there were several generations of increasing stability, during which some of the advantages of Roman civilization were recovered, without its artistic dullness. Bede, one of the greatest historians of the middle ages, who worked in Northumbria at the time the *Lindisfarne Gospels* were produced there, says that in King Edwin's day, a hundred years before his own, there was such perfect peace in Edwin's kingdom that, in the words of the proverb, a woman with her new-born babe might walk from sea to sea unharmed.

Pls. 14, 15

Augustine's mission was to Kent, and its effects were limited. But it was followed in the second half of the following century by a mission that was more ambitious in its scope, and which, as Bede's account shows, was concerned not only to convert the heathen but to educate him. The two men who led this

[8]

Plate 2

THE LION OF ST. MARK

From the Book of Durrow. Northumbrian, c. 670 A.D. *See p. 48* they begin to appear, even in the decoration of books, before the full 'Hiberno-Saxon' style is developed. The trumpet spirals, on which the magnificent design of Plate 10 (b) is based, are Celtic, and pre-Roman, in origin, but they had been adopted by the Anglo-Saxon metal-workers, and are known on a great series of hanging bowls found in Anglo-Saxon graves and dating from before the Sutton Hoo period. The intricate geometric patterns built up from small units, like those on the chequered body of the lion in Plate 2, are derived from Anglo-Saxon cloisonné work, in which each section of colour is divided from the next by raised lines of metal, forming compartments that are filled with the enamel paste of the separate colours.

Compare the boars of Pl. 52b

What is not explained from any of these sources is the strange treatment of the human figure, wrapped often in great rolls of stuff, the limbs and features conventionalized to a remarkable degree—a treatment that is the very antithesis of the classical tradition, and may perhaps, if it is not a Northumbrian invention, be Irish. At any rate in the earliest of the books it does not appear, and the only attempt at a human figure in the *Book of Durrow* (the symbol for the Evangelist Matthew) wears a cloak as it were of chequered enamel like the body of the lion in Plate 2, both this and the head and features of the figure being quite uncharacteristic of the later Irish style. This ordinary 'Irish' style of representing the human figure is not here illustrated, for the evangelists in the *Lindisfarne Gospels* are only partly barbaric in their ancestry. It has been shown that they owe much to classical originals which can be proved to have been available to the artist who made them.

Pl. 15a, b

The intrusion of an Irish element into Anglo-Saxon art (if indeed this is such an intrusion) would need explanation, and that explanation may furnish us with a clue to the immediate stimulus of the movement. St. Patrick's mission to Ireland had led eventually to the foundation of a series of monasteries in Ireland which gradually acquired, in the early middle ages, a reputation for enormous learning. So far as can be now made out, this learning was of a curiously crabbed variety, and expended its resources on strange linguistic tricks rather than on intelligent or original speculation; and the much vaunted acquaintance with Greek may have meant little more at this time than is shown by the artist of Plate 15 who uses the Greek words *O Agios Iohannes* (St. John) as part of his decorative design. But if Irish learning in the early middle ages did not amount to very much by later standards, there can be no doubt of the stimulus which it provided. According to Bede, many Englishmen of distinguished, and not so distinguished, families left Northumbria and went to live in Irish monasteries in the mid-seventh century to study; and were welcomed, and given the wherewithal freely, both food and books, for a life of study. Bede's account of the period gives indeed the impression that it was their strictness of life which gave the Irish missionaries a pre-eminent reputation, but though Ireland itself is for him a barbarous land, he frequently emphasizes their devotion to the study of the scriptures. Thus when Ireland began to repay the debt she owed for St. Patrick's mission by missionary activities in Scotland, spreading from St. Columba's foundation on the Island of Iona, the stimulus brought to the religious communities of Northern England, newly established by teachers coming from the South, was great. The Irish missionaries provided new views on what

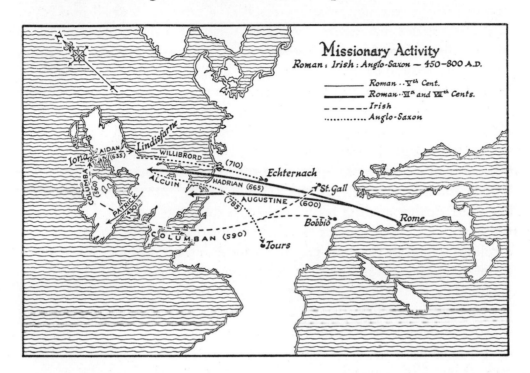

Missionary Activity
Roman: Irish: Anglo-Saxon — 450–800 A.D.

————— Roman ·· Vᵗʰ Cent.
————— Roman · VIᵗʰ and VIIᵗʰ Cents.
– – – – – Irish
············· Anglo-Saxon

were regarded as vital topics—in particular on the method of tonsure and the date of Easter, on which much of the Christian calendar depended. It seems incredible that such discussions should have been a stimulating influence. But the records of the time leave no doubt about it. The Irish brought also a new series of texts, including a text of the Latin New Testament with certain variations to it. And so, even if the great artistic movement of which the *Lindisfarne* *Pls. 14, 15* *Gospels* is the masterpiece, did not originate in Ireland, nor was it derived solely, if indeed at all, from Ireland, Northumbria was the meeting place of a number of cultural influences, from Ireland, from England, and through England, from Italy. It was this meeting of different streams which gave the artistic movement its force. It is not surprising that in Bede Northumbria should have produced the greatest scholar of the early middle ages, and in the *Lindisfarne Gospels* perhaps the greatest book of the early middle ages; nor that Charlemagne at the end of the eighth century should have sent to Northumbria for his schoolmasters. For in this period Northumbrian civilization has a clear primacy. And when the tide flows back to Ireland, taking with it the motives of Anglo-Saxon art, the great period is almost over, and the *Book of Kells* itself, though it is unrivalled in Western Europe as a monument of human ingenuity and patience, may perhaps be considered less successful as a work of art than its Northumbrian prototype, the *Lindisfarne Gospels*.

Appendix I

We have material for forming some idea of the books produced on the continent in the centuries preceding the *Book of Durrow*. A small number of classical illustrated manuscripts, copies of Virgil, or books of the Bible with narrative illustrations describing the story found in the text, survives. The tradition of these classical books (one example of which, intimately connected with the early missionaries in England, we have examined above) descends into the figure drawings of the Carolingian and later medieval schools, and is of great importance. But what is new in the Northumbrian books, and is in complete contrast with classical narrative illustration, is the idea of many pages of sheer decoration, of patterns made up of geometric forms, or of animals which, while they are astonishingly lively, are yet utterly unlike any actual living specimen. The chief quality of these books, indeed, is the artists' power of combining pattern with life. Their patterns are of extraordinary elaboration and are painted in colours which are the more satisfactory for their sober delicacy. The symbolism of the great cruciform pages of decoration in the copies of the Gospels, the symbol of the cross which seems to impose order and pattern on the wild vitality of a barbaric imagination, would be inescapable if we did not get something comparable in the jewellery which has no Christian inspiration. In any event, the first phase of medieval art draws its character from this unrivalled decorative work, from which source is ultimately derived the purely decorative work in the books of the Middle Ages.

Pl. 53b

Pls. 9, 10, 12-14

Pls. 13, 14

Pl. 52a, b

The distribution of Irish and Anglo-Saxon books throughout Western Europe is an index of the power of the missionary movement in the seventh and eighth centuries. From the North Italian monastery of Bobbio comes a whole series of Irish seventh century books. But they are without decoration, and written with little regard for the beauty of the page. It is notable too that many of them are written on rubbed-out copies of classical texts for which the Irish monks had no use. They were not leaders of a renaissance, but preachers of asceticism. When we come to the age of the Anglo-Saxon missionaries like St. Willibrord, who worked in Germany in the eighth century, there is a change. A splendid copy of the Gospels that belonged to St. Willibrord himself and comes from his monastery of Echternach, can be taken as an example. Willibrord was a Northumbrian, and his book is from the same scriptorium as the *Book of Durrow*. Its Anglo-Saxon—as opposed to Irish—character can be demonstrated with

Pl. 11, 52c, 53a

certainty. Our plate shows the lion of St. Mark, a superbly savage beast, ram- *Pl. 11*
pant over the page. This style was eventually to spread to the Irish monasteries
on the continent also, and there are fine Irish books from St. Gall in Switzerland
decorated in it. But they are later than the Northumbrian manuscripts from which
their decoration was derived.

In the south of England the Northumbrian style had an important influence. But classical tradition was not overwhelmed as it was in Northumbria.
Thus we find being produced in Canterbury a psalter decorated with a minia- *Pl. 53c*
ture of King David playing the harp and various others playing instruments of
the orchestra, a theme perhaps suggested by the introduction into England of
Italian Church music described by Bede. The figure drawing is a native version
of classical, as is another illumination, probably by the same hand, in a copy *cf. p. 38*
of the Gospels, from Canterbury, now in Stockholm. Many of the ornamental *Pl. 53a*
motifs in both these books are Northumbrian, like the spirals in the frame of the
David page, but the predominant effect is of debased classical work. And when
at the court of Charlemagne an attempt was made to revive classical culture in
general, it was natural that this classical style, rather than the magnificent barbaric work of Northumbria, should be favoured, just as it was natural for
Alcuin's followers in Tours—even though Alcuin had brought them from
Northumbria—to make copies of classical manuscripts such as the Irishmen at
Bobbio had destroyed. The achievements of Carolingian artists rapidly became
predominant in Western Europe. It looks as if there were one artist of genius who
infused new life into the classical style, so that his figures are not mere dolls, like
the Canterbury David, but living creatures, caught by the artist's eye as it were *Pls. 53c, 54d*
in an actual moment of time. From him is ultimately derived the brilliant work
of the Rheims ninth century artists through whose drawings the classical tradition was to pass back to England in a new form in the tenth century. Meanwhile
in the far north the old style continued to be practised. From Iona at the end of
the ninth century, comes a book still decorated in the Northumbrian style. And
in Irish art of the late middle ages the tradition lives on, and is represented by
many magnificent examples of craftsmanship; whereas in the south, so much
more receptive to new influences, it had long been forgotten.

IV

The Late Anglo-Saxon Period

In the ninth century the comparative peace of Anglo-Saxon England was broken by the disastrous invasions of Vikings and Danes. 'It has come to my remembrance' writes Alfred the Great 'what wise men there were formerly among the English race, both of the sacred orders and of the secular, and what happy times there were throughout the English race, and how the kings, who had the Government of God, in those days obeyed God and his ministers. I remembered also how the churches throughout all England stood filled with treasures and with books.' But already before the Viking invasions learning had begun to decline. There might be books, but there were few, says Alfred, any longer who could understand them, and if the historians are right in the order in which they arrange the books that have come down to us, the latest of these early Anglo-Saxon books show a long decline from the consummate artistry of the *Lindisfarne Gospels*. The Viking invasions brought to an end a culture which for some reason appears to have been already dying.

To the fertility and poise of Alfred's own mind was largely due the recreation of literature and education. But the books surviving from his day are not, generally speaking, decorated. Alfred died in 901 and our second phase does not begin till the last third of this new century. It seems to originate in a revival of monastic life associated with Aethelwold, Bishop of Winchester. Many books of this period have been called 'Winchester' books because they have stylistic *Pl. 3* links with the famous *Benedictional of St. Aethelwold*, even where there is no evi- *Note vi* dence that they were actually made in Winchester. But some of the finest undoubtedly were, and if the first period is Northumbrian the original focus of this second period of illumination is in the South; though from its brilliant beginnings the tradition spread, so that in the early years of the eleventh century work *Pls. 16, 20,* of fine quality was being provided for (and perhaps in) monasteries as far afield *55b, c* as Bury St. Edmunds, Peterborough, York and Durham. 'Monasticism in the West', wrote Harnack, 'made history, secular and religious alike.' In Winchester, the capital of late Anglo-Saxon England, there were two great monasteries at this time, the Priory of St. Swithun (the church of which, rebuilt in Norman times and altered in later centuries, is the present cathedral) and the New Minster,

Plate 3

THE ASCENDING CHRIST

Above are angels holding the instruments of the Passion

From the Benedictional of St. Aethelwold, Bishop of Winchester. Winchester, c. 980 A.D. See p. 43

which at this time stood adjacent to the Priory of St. Swithun. From both of these there survive books of magnificent quality. And there is little doubt that it is the monastic revival of Aethelwold, a reformation which affected particularly the moral and religious life of the monasteries, which brings these late Anglo-Saxon artists into existence and makes their work so different from that done fifty years before—that work of Athelstan's reign which offers such great archaeological interest and so little aesthetic satisfaction.

In this late period of Anglo-Saxon art is seen the continuity in art of the classical tradition. It is entirely different from the 'barbaric' Anglo-Saxon art of the Northumbrian period. We have noticed already that books had been illustrated, rather than decorated, by the late classical artists. In some late Anglo-Saxon drawings can be seen the revival of this narrative tradition, but in a fresh, *Pls. 20-22* lively and delicate new form. Thus they differ from the classical books themselves, *55b, c* and are less coarse and clumsy than the work executed after the classical tradition by continental artists of the generations following Charlemagne. But whereas the Northumbrian School sprang into existence seemingly out of nothing, the Winchester School owes much to these continental artists—such as the artists of the *Utrecht Psalter* (who seem to have worked in the Rheims district) or the designer of the Lothair crystal. Their drawings (in spite of the *Pl. 55a* strange mannerisms in which artist follows artist so slavishly, the curved, jointless *Pls. 16, 17,* fingers or the hunched and distorted shoulders) are full of life and movement. *20, 22* They are often heightened with colour, or executed in coloured inks, and their *Pl. 4* effect often depends on this and on rapid characterization, achieved by a few lines or by the poise of the body which tells, with remarkable economy, what the artist wishes to say. The draperies are dainty and fluttering, an extraordinary contrast to the fixed patterns of the *Lindisfarne Gospels*, and there is often a smile—sometimes an incongruous smile—over the lips. Many of the drawings indeed have real gaiety and humour, and as Alfred the Great's writings give the impression of a humanism and inquisitiveness almost unparalleled in any period between the fall of the Roman Empire and the Renaissance, so these drawings, belonging to the age which his reign made possible, have none of the oppressive seriousness of some medieval work, and are at the same time more adult than the delightful but childlike drawings of the fourteenth and fifteenth centuries. *Pl. 42*

There were produced in a different style some magnificent service books. The immediate inspiration for these books comes from an increased attention to ceremonial which was characteristic of the reforms of Cluny, and which reached England through the medium of Fleury with which Aethelwold had close connexions. Thus we have from the period not only copies of the Gospels intended for ceremonial use, but Benedictionals, Pontificals, and Sacramentaries such as are without parallel in the early Anglo-Saxon period. The effect

[15]

of this inspiration was lasting. From now onwards, service books will concern us extensively. In the 'Winchester School' books of this time a feature of the *Pl. 3* decorated pages is the enclosing of the main design in a double frame filled with foliage; which often spreads luxuriantly and intertwines to form a lavish and splendid pattern. The pictures set in these frames are of course more formal than the outline drawings. They anticipate the severe and dignified treatment *Pls. 16, 17* of a later age. Some designs, particularly of the Evangelists of the gospel books, lie halfway between the narrative and decorative styles, having the freshness and delicacy of the outline drawings disciplined with a greater severity. And where, as in one copy of the Gospels from the New Minster at Winchester, *Pls. 18, 19* the frame is filled not with foliage but with a great pattern of Angels' wings, the result is masterly. Between the *Lindisfarne Gospels* and these late Anglo-Saxon books, like the *Grimbald Gospels* and the *Benedictional of St. Aethelwold*, there is as we have seen a break in the tradition—a break pointed out by Dr. Eric Millar in the preface to his book on English illumination of the tenth to twelfth centuries. But these late books of the Winchester School lie at the veritable beginning of English art, and the line from them forward to the East *Pls. 3-8, 16-* Anglian books of the early fourteenth century or to the *Queen Mary Psalter* is *50* unbroken.

Plate 4

FRONTISPIECE TO THE LIBER VITAE OF
THE NEW MINSTER

Showing King Canute and Queen Aelfgyfu presenting a gold cross
Above, Christ in a mandorla, flanked by the Virgin and St. Peter
Below, monks

New Minster, Winchester, c. 1020 A.D. See p. 45

V

The Romanesque Period

Though the tradition is continuous from the work of the Winchester School to the fifteenth century the style passes through various phases and by the middle of the twelfth century we are aware that a new age is in being. The second of the two great periods of the medieval epoch, periods which we attempted to define at the outset, has begun, and with it have come new values in art as well as in learning. The twelfth century is in some ways the greatest, in all ways the most ambitious period in the history of English illumination. For what was characteristic of the work done now was not simply its precision, its accuracy under the magnifying glass, which was to be equalled and probably surpassed in the later periods as it had been at the time of the *Lindisfarne Gospels*. Nor does the difference lie simply in the disappearance of the brilliant sketches of Anglo-Saxon artists, though it is true that the faces drawn by the twelfth century artists tend to become types and the figures to lose the wild abandon with which the Anglo-Saxon figure flings out a gesture or is whirled upon a wheel. But the artist is thinking in new terms—severity, dignity, power. This is the one phase in which gaiety is avoided. In the Anglo-Saxon drawings it is often part and parcel of the main theme. In later work of the thirteenth and fourteenth centuries the artist again and again becomes preoccupied with the by-plot. His main drawing may be a Last Judgment or the Son seated at the right hand of the Father, yet on the same page is a drawing of a monkey hunting an owl, a drawing that might be a decoration not for the Psalter but for Aesop's Fables; or something coarser, designed it would almost seem to remind us that we must not look on the middle ages as the innocent childhood of Western Europe, but as a civilization in its own right, mature and complex, knowing good and evil. In the twelfth century these by-plots have hardly begun, and while the artist may elaborate the frame with superbly rich decoration, there is a single intention. These Romanesque artists, almost always severe in drawing, are in their mood always stern. It is the exception for any tenderness to be allowed a place. On a larger scale their work must have been sometimes awesome or even tragic in its intensity.

Pls. 20, 21
Pls. 5, 23, 25
27, 28

Pl. 40

Pls. 25b, 28

Thus in the books of the twelfth century English art reaches a pinnacle of achievement which outsoared the rest because its aims were loftier. We may agree that, like so many medieval structures, it proved to be too ambitious; that the artist of the greatest twelfth century books was trying to achieve something on a surface of square inches that could never be fully achieved except on a surface measured in square feet; that he forgot that his job was to decorate a book, moved as he was by the grandeur of ideas which were material for far more than decoration. In the few square inches of a drawing showing the en-

Pl. 30 tombment of Judas Maccabaeus from the *Winchester Bible* we find an emotional
Pl. 23 content almost as profound as in the great wall painting of St. Paul at Canterbury. The lightness and airiness of the Anglo-Saxon artist has vanished. The draughtsman's line is still, at its best, of wonderful purity. But the smile has been replaced by a frown, gaiety by anxiety, facility by rigorous severity. The charac-
Pls. 24, 25 teristic representation of drapery is not free and fluttering, but highly formalized, reduced to a pattern which is in strict harmony with the pattern of the whole design. Movement, when there is movement, is concentrated on a strict purpose.
Pl. 5 The music of the heavens has become a solemn music. The shepherds are bewildered and stunned by the vision of angels, and the glory and majesty of God begins to be realized as something that is no longer to be expressed in terms of charming and eager human figures. William Blake would have found himself at home among the artists who decorated the *Lambeth Bible*, for they, like Blake, had become aware of the sublimity of God, meting out the heavens with a span, and setting bounds to the waters which they must not pass.

What was it that brought this new character into the work of the twelfth century? Artistically, it was probably contacts with Byzantine art, with manuscripts in the first instance and later almost certainly with mosaics also. Sicily
Note vii was a meeting place of East and West, and the English court had contacts with Sicily in the course of the century. Henry of Blois, Bishop of Winchester, who was a notable patron of the arts, travelled to Italy more than once. In a psalter from St. Swithun's Priory made during his episcopacy there are two pages which have been claimed as the work of an 'Italo-Byzantine' artist. Mr. Wormald has suggested that they are by an English artist who had a Byzantine original in his mind, and in the *Winchester Bible* there is also to be found work with close
Note viii Byzantine analogies. We know of works of art being brought to Winchester from the continent in Henry of Blois' time, including sculpture and enamel, and it would be surprising if English art did not show traces of foreign contacts during the century of the Crusades.

What is doubtless still more important is the change brought about in the intellectual climate by the revival of learning. The widening range of subject is one sign of this. Before this time there is a long series of evangelists—treated with

Plate 5

THE ANGELS AND THE SHEPHERDS

(The colour has been partly scraped off, doubtless for use elsewhere)

Old Minster, Winchester, c. 1140 A.D. See p. 45

great variety it is true; and only occasionally in the Psalter do we get extensive narrative drawing. There are a few New Testament scenes, associated with particular feasts (as the entry to Jerusalem was associated with Palm Sunday). But the twelfth century artist begins to illustrate an enormous variety of scenes from both the Old and the New Testaments. He is beginning to be familiar with the text in great detail. Moreover, as we have seen, there were now becoming available translations from the Greek. This first impact of the classics—infiltration is a more exact word for it—shows itself not so much in any humanism of thought or of art, as in just this increase of intellectuality; in the establishing of the tremendous prestige of intellectual authority as against independent speculation; in a self-conscious seriousness of outlook. A copy of *Terence* in the Bodleian Library at Oxford, on which worked one of the artists of the *Winchester* *Pl. 56c* *Bible*, may be taken as a symbol of this attitude. It was made from a classical original, of which an earlier copy is still in existence, so that we know the little figures in their simple classical tunics and cloaks, and their comic masks, which the twelfth century artist had before him. The loose classical folds are replaced by the elaborate formal patterns of the twelfth century. The mask has become something grim and terrifying. In these two books two worlds are in direct touch, but the later grotesquely misunderstands the earlier. So classical learning in the twelfth century was absorbed into a new synthesis which the Greeks and Romans would have found utterly incomprehensible. Aristotle would no more have recognized the interpretation of his views in the Schools of the twelfth century than Terence would have recognized the actors of the *Bodleian Terence*. But it is true nevertheless to say that classical ideas are of great importance in both spheres. Classical sculpture certainly exercises an influence on much Gothic sculpture. The influence of classical design on medieval English books is indeed insignificant (except where there is a Byzantine intermediary) and when we see a Gorgon's head incorporated into a decorated border, it is some- *Note ix* thing of a problem to know whether it is an independent invention, or how it came to be there. But the influence of the new learning on the general climate of thought was profound, and as Englishmen like John of Salisbury and Adelard of Bath were pioneers in the rediscovery of classical logic and mathematics, it need cause us no surprise that the greatest English artists of this age, like the master of the Canterbury St. Paul, are pioneers also, and pioneers whose work *Pl. 23* is of superlative quality. This Romanesque period, with its work so solemn, so formal, and so dignified, is the third phase in our sequence.

VI

The Early Gothic Period

The fourth phase reaches its climax in the East Anglian books of the early fourteenth century. The change from Romanesque to Gothic art has taken place, and with it has come a tenderness, and also a softness, that was alien to Romanesque art. To show this, a detail may be taken which has had to be considerably enlarged for our purpose, and naturally has lost in the process something of its miniature charm. It portrays the cruxifixion, and in his *Pl. 31* representation of three separate moments, the artist has turned his back, as it were, on the eternal, and fixed his attention on the temporal. In the first of the three moments, shown in the upper scene, the Christ is alive and looking down with seeing eyes on his mockers. In the second, the head has begun to droop, the arms have lost their strength, and if the eyes are still open, the spirit of life is ebbing. In the third the exhausted body is limp and is hanging by the arms, for death has now closed the eyes. Thus in place of a scene treated as symbolical of the theological truth, the symbol of redemption, it is now treated as a sequence of human events. The emphasis has shifted from the divinity of Christ to the humanity of Christ, and while (for example) the characteristic theme chosen by one sculptor after another in the twelfth century is a Christ in majesty, in the thirteenth and fourteenth centuries it is Christ suffering on the Cross. Similarly, though representation of the Virgin and Child is not unknown in the Roman-*Pls. 6, 38, 46,* esque period, in the Gothic period it becomes much more frequent. These *47* changes, accompanied with a growing naturalism that shows itself most readily probably in the changing treatment of drapery, alter the whole character of the art of the period. A 'prettiness' and grace soon show themselves, which make this Gothic art easier to grasp, even if it is less profound, than the Romanesque; and the full development of these qualities is the mannered East Anglian school *Pls. 34-39* in which there is a danger of art becoming 'art for art's sake'.

Here also if we cannot give actual reasons for the change between Roman-esque and Gothic, we can at least attempt a somewhat deeper analysis which shows it as part of a much bigger change. 'Real changes in human sentiment,' wrote Mr. C. S. Lewis in his *Allegory of Love*, 'are very rare—there are probably

[20]

Plate 6

VIRGIN AND CHILD; ON EITHER SIDE AN ANGEL CENSING

(The silver used for details, including the two censers, has oxidised)

Chichester, Bishop's Palace (wall painting), c. 1250 A.D. See p. 47

three or four of them on record—but I believe that they occur, and that this is one of them.' He is talking of the discovery or invention, or at least the first expression, by French poets in the eleventh century of that romantic species of passion which English poets were still writing about in the nineteenth. He points out that there is no evidence of the quasi-religious tone of medieval love poetry being transferred from the worship of the Blessed Virgin. 'It is just as likely—it is even more likely—that the colouring of certain hymns to the Virgin has been borrowed from the love poetry.' During the thirteenth century this ideal of romantic love and courtly chivalry begins to become part of English life, finding its literary expression as the legends of King Arthur and his knights were elaborated (the original inspiration here also coming largely from France) and having as one of its by-products the rich heraldry often used as a decorative motif in the manuscripts of the early fourteenth century. If the roundel painting of the Virgin and Child *Pl. 6* at Chichester is compared with a Byzantine Virgin, the reality of the change is strikingly seen. The Byzantine Virgin seems to stand at the head of a hierarchy, at the right hand of a son who has already entered his glory. She is not a mother leaning over her child. The Italian Virgins of this same period, though they are shown with the Christ-Child, have hardly lost this hieratic character. But the Virgin of the Chichester roundel belongs already to two worlds, the human as well as the divine, and the loveliness of motherhood is at the heart of the artist's purpose. It is a breath of humanism which in English art was to become clouded and frozen; and the charm of the convention formed in the process cannot blind us to the gradual loss of real feeling—so that the artist is driven to assert his humanity in the by-plots that have been mentioned above. His work at the moment when the tension between the two tendencies is at its greatest, one tending towards naturalism, the other towards a sort of other-worldly formalism or childlike daintiness, is of extraordinary beauty, and for this reason it would be tempting to claim the St. Michael of Plate 35 as the masterpiece of medieval illustrators.

VII

The Conditions in which Illuminated Books were Produced

Note x It is not surprising that East Anglia should in the early fourteenth century have been the centre of artistic production in England, for the latter part of the Early Gothic period coincides with a period of unparalleled wealth in East Anglia, due to the prosperity of the wool trade at the time. The decline coincides with further economic changes in the region. This point draws our attention to the increasing importance of technical questions, questions of market and method of production, in the history of illumination in later medieval times.

We know as yet little for certain about the conditions under which illuminated books were produced, though some important books carry inscriptions which relate to their production, for these inscriptions can too often be interpreted in various ways. If a particular twelfth century book was in a particular monastery in the twelfth century, is that satisfactory evidence that it was produced there, or were books often produced in one monastery for another? We do not know. When did the production of books by commercial scribes, even for monastic use, become usual? We can give only a tentative answer. If a man claims to be the *scriptor* of a book, we do not know whether he wrote the text, designed or completed the decorations, or was responsible for all these things. We seldom know anything of his status and seldom even his name.

One thing however may be asserted confidently. From the eighth to the fifteenth century there continue to be instances of books being produced and decorated by clerics, and in the earliest period the evidence suggests that all were *Pls. 14, 15* so produced. The famous inscription in the *Lindisfarne Gospels* indicates that the book was written (and we may by inference also say illuminated, since the inscription seems intended to give full details) by Eadfrith, Bishop of Lindisfarne 698-721 'in honour of God and of St. Cuthbert and all the saints in common who are on the island'. The book was bound by Aethelwold, Bishop of Lindisfarne, 724-740—and the form of words used, 'bound it, as he was able to do', seems to imply that he did not simply pay for the binding, but that the

Plate 7

A SAINT, PERHAPS AN EVANGELIST

From the Oscott Psalter, XIIIth Century, last quarter. *See p. 48*

actual execution of the work was carried out with his own hands. A jewelled cover was then made for it by Billfrith the Anchorite. At this time, therefore, expert craftsmanship might naturally go with a high position in the Church, and during the Northumbrian period most books were undoubtedly produced in, and for, monasteries.

There is nothing to suggest that in this early Anglo-Saxon period the copying of books played anything like the part in monastic life which it was to play later. When St. Benedict composed his *Rule* early in the sixth century, a rule which was widely if not universally followed in Western Europe in the following centuries, he reckoned on the likelihood that many of the monastery's inmates would be illiterate. It is true that he enjoins on his monks the importance of writing, but characteristically the injunction is connected especially with Lent, and the implication clearly is that they might find thereby a suitable penance for the good of their souls. As has been pointed out above, it is the great development of ceremonial in the tenth century that inspires the illumination of the late Anglo-Saxon 'Winchester' school. And owing to the conditions of the time, and in particular to the frequent movement of individuals or groups from monastery to monastery, it is unusually difficult to be certain where a book was produced in that period.

As to some conditions of production, however, the *Benedictional of St. Aethel-* *wold* contains useful evidence in the form of a description, in some detail, of orders given by this later Aethelwold, Bishop of Winchester, for the writing and decoration of the book, which was made for his ceremonial use. The 'writer' (*scriptor*) named Goodman, was in one of the monasteries in Aethelwold's diocese—possibly in the New Minster at Winchester. There is nothing positively to show that the decoration of the book, as opposed to the writing of the text, was done in the monastery. But it is a fair assumption, and indeed one in the list of distinguished monks of the New Minster is described as 'painter and priest', and long after this we still find artists who hold some position in the church. During the next four hundred years, however, it became usual for illuminations to be executed by outside craftsmen, even when the work was being done for monastic patrons. About 1400, there was produced a splendid missal apparently for Sherborne, of which the scribe and the chief illuminator were a Benedictine monk and a Dominican friar. But this illuminator may reasonably be regarded also as a professional artist. He certainly worked in various places, and there is, in later medieval times in England, nothing to correspond with the monastic school of illumination. Already in the twelfth century can be discerned the beginnings of a system by which a monastery might set aside funds (as did Abbot Simon of St. Albans in the second half of the twelfth century) for the payment of artists, presumably professional artists, to work on fine books. The

Pl. 3

Note xi

cf. above, p. 10

cf. Pls. 5, 25
(the artist of
Pls. 27, 28)

Pl. 42

Note xii
Pl. 25b

work of one of the *Winchester Bible* artists occurs in a book that was already in the twelfth century at St. Albans, the *Bodleian Terence*. Thus even in the Romanesque period the work of the monastic schools of artists might be supplemented by that of itinerant professional artists. From twelfth century Winchester, however, there is a series of books carrying similar decoration and showing undoubted development within one tradition, and we might be justified in calling this a school, even though it excludes one of the most notable of the Bible artists. A school of Bury St. Edmunds at the time is also recognizable, perhaps also one of Canterbury. In the twelfth century, therefore, the situation seems to have been complex. There were some local monastic schools, but their work was supplemented by that of professional artists travelling from place to place.

By the time of the *Tickhill Psalter*, produced in the early fourteenth century, there were apparently groups of artists consisting of three or four members, travelling from one job to the next, like the stone masons of East Anglia, whom Dr. Coulton describes. But by this date another change had taken place, a change in the market. Though Tickyll himself was an Abbot, the artists' patrons are now more often rich laymen than monks. And illuminated books were certainly being produced by scribes working to order, in their own workshops in the cities. In the thirteenth century some University towns on the continent had guilds of scribes, with a fixed tariff of charges. In Paris in the mid-fifteenth century the guild known as the *Confrèrie de St. Jean l'Evangéliste* included scribes, binders and illuminators. Many of the not very good fifteenth century illuminated service books and Books of Hours were undoubtedly turned out by such urban bookshops, and by methods which might fairly be called mass production. This change in the market—from the Church to the *bourgeois* merchant—and in the *atelier*—from the scriptorium of the monastery to the bookshops of London or Oxford or wherever it might be—coincides with a notable decline in quality. Briefly then, it may be said that in the Anglo-Saxon and Romanesque periods we are dealing largely with monastic production, in later medieval times either with travelling groups of artists or with urban bookshops, and that between these systems there was a considerable degree of overlapping. And in terms of our series of illustrations this means that every book illustrated from the early fourteenth century onwards, except the *Tickhill Psalter*, appears to have been made for a layman, not for a religious house.

It is to be noted, also, that the attitude of the artist was less individualistic than modern analogies might suggest. There are, in the *Winchester Bible*, many examples of paintings in which the design was made by one artist and completed by another. In at least one initial the faces were completed by a different artist from the man who painted the rest. In the *Tickhill Psalter* we find one artist working on the main subject of the full illuminated page, another on the

Plate 8

CHRIST IN MAJESTY

Holding in His hand the orb of the world divided into three continents

In the four corners of the page, the four evangelists with their symbols

Considerably reduced, from the Psalter of Robert de Lisle. East Anglian XIVth Century, end of first quarter. *See p. 48*

little drawings at the foot of it, with what is presumably the more important artist adding an occasional group of figures to the sketches at the foot. And the unfinished state in which this book, and many others, have been left shows that it was not the practice to carry one page through to completion, but rather to work in stages, a first, a second and a third or finishing stage, and to carry through the first stage on a number of leaves before the second was begun anywhere. These stages may sometimes still have been the work of different craftsmen, as they undoubtedly were with some initials of the *Winchester Bible*.

We can trace moreover in some twelfth century books (such as the *Canterbury Psalter*) the assistant working side by side with the master, using the same formulas but with a much cruder touch, and in many twelfth century initials the work of master and assistant is no doubt mixed beyond the possibility of disentangling the two. The illuminated page was often a co-operative work. Two or three men often contributed to the final result. So in the pair of initials at the head of the *Psalms* in the *Winchester Bible*, the movement of the 'leaping   *Pl. 26* figures' betrays what can readily be demonstrated from other details, a design in the hand of an artist other than the man who completed it. Both these two were masters, and they were working on a book which both of them must have known would be one of the masterpieces of its day. But the practice of committing to the craftsman one stage only in the finished painting might well eventually lead to the attitude of the manufacturer rather than the artist, and this may have been one factor in the decline of standards in the later medieval period. If a man's job was simply to put on the undercoating of the faces, and if the destination of his book depended on whether the next customer in the shop wanted the most expensive style or not, his work was likely to be of a different character from that of a man working on a book for his own monastery.

Almost all the illuminated books here illustrated are splendid examples. But the work in scores of others is often rough, and is sometimes crude. What it is not, however (in these earlier periods) is shoddy. That is a feature of the bad fifteenth century books, and is doubtless a function of the changing market and changed conditions of production. For if books up to that time had never been shoddy, other things had. There is an Anglo-Saxon lead brooch, or pin, in the library of Winchester Cathedral, which is as bad as any piece of jewellery that ever came out of a Christmas cracker—indeed, is considerably worse, because it has not the gaudy brightness of cracker jewellery. It has to be kept safely locked up in a drawer, in case the general public, knowing that it is Anglo-Saxon, might think that they ought to admire it. Brooches in the time of Aethelwold and Canute evidently commanded a market that books did not. It was worth producing them for people who could not distinguish good and bad. In the fifteenth century it began to be a mark of gentility to own a Book of

Hours. And so, though some books of high quality and fine workmanship are still produced, yet most of them fail to give the sense of achievement which the greatest wall-paintings or the occasional good pieces of sculpture still give. The focus was shifting and it was no longer usual for the artist of talent to look here for his opportunities. The journeyman could do as well all that the public wanted, while the connoisseur bought his books in France or Italy or Flanders.

VIII

The Late Gothic Period

The last period, our 'late Gothic' period, passes through two distinct stages, between which it ought perhaps to be definitely subdivided. In the first, all the figures that the artist draws have a childlike air of simplicity about them. The series of drawings in the *Tickhill Psalter* that narrate *Pl. 42* the history of King David provides an example. Saul, David, their generals, their retainers and their wives all appear to be children playing a game. There is no hint of mature emotions working below the surface; and whereas in the period immediately preceding this, the great East Anglian artists vented their less respectable emotions on the margins, we are led sometimes to suspect that these artists had no depths of feeling; that they were playing with engaging superficialities, doing so with a lightness of touch that has not often been surpassed—but *Pls. 43-45* nevertheless playing. This tendency reaches its climax in the *Queen Mary Psalter*. In it the workmanship is fine, and the taste impeccable, so that the artist seems at first to have high claims. But the judgment may be hazarded that, charming though his work is, it nevertheless falls short of greatness. It is more than pretty. There is a loveliness about it and an underlying seriousness, which make it more important than most of the comparable English books. But it knows nothing of the depths of human emotion, of sorrow, or of pity, or of joy, because it does not belong to the world of human emotions at all, but to a world of make-believe.

What brings about a change is the first promise of the Renaissance. For while books which were purely medieval in ideas and treatment continued to be produced to the end of the fifteenth century yet in the greatest books the signs of the times are unmistakable. The pretty, unreal creatures of the second quarter of the fourteenth century become men and women of flesh and blood. The modelling of the flesh is three dimensional. In the *Ormesby Psalter*, belonging to *Pls. 40, 41* the early years of the fourteenth century, there had been already an extraordinary anticipation of this. Many of the figures, especially those of the margins, are Renaissance figures. The old, and typically medieval, censorship of nakedness begins to be discarded. It is typical that, even in the *Tickhill Psalter*, there is a series of flower drawings in which many species are identifiable, being evidently drawn from life; and typical also that this had happened some time before in sculpture, even in England—on the sculptured leaves adorning the capitals of Southwell Minster. In France (for during this Gothic period the leadership was with France) such naturalistic foliage had been used by sculptors still earlier.

An Annunciation, painted in the first years of the fifteenth century, can be taken to illustrate the progress of this general tendency. The new treatment of flesh makes it seem alive, and there is a new understanding of human feeling. Here it seems to be the feeling of awe, and of acceptance, of humility and pride. This same picture perhaps illustrates also a point made above, the division of labour between craftsman and craftsman. A frame so perfunctory could hardly have been given to a picture so good, by the man who painted the picture. If the border were the work of another hand, this strange disparity between them would be explained.

cf. above, p. 25

The quality of the finest fifteenth century painting lies in the fusion of medieval and Renaissance minds. The fine illuminations from the *Hours of Elizabeth the Queene* will illustrate this. From their medieval predecessors these artists inherit grace, simplicity and faith. From the Renaissance comes awareness of the body as something beautiful, and a responsiveness to human feelings—the feelings, not of children but of adults. In his figure of the penitent thief the artist explores a new emotional interest, typical of the new age. In a figure such as that of Peter in the scene of the Arrest, there is a moving conflict between the old and the new. Peter unmistakably means business. His sword is drawn and the ear is indeed already off that offensive face. And yet Peter is obviously too simple still for the bewilderingly complicated and wicked world in which he finds himself. His stoutness of heart is the courage of the loyal child. In such a tension between the old world and the new, the great works also of the Italian fifteenth century artists were produced.

Pls. 49, 50

Pl. 50

Pl. 49

It remains true, however, that changing conditions have by this time affected the artistic quality of almost all the books produced. The customer was often without discrimination, and was content if the decoration of a book was elaborate, or effective, or looked reasonably expensive. This does not imply a general decline in the arts. An age which produced the Nave of Canterbury Cathedral need not fear comparisons. Richard II was a noteworthy patron of the arts, in whose reign not only great architecture, like the roof of Westminster Hall, but also great painting, like the *Wilton Diptych*—or if it be objected that the English origin of that is uncertain, let us take the marvellous glass of Thomas Glazier of Oxford—was produced. It would be hard to find drawing more lovely, even in France, than that of Thomas Glazier's Virgin and Child, here reproduced. But the flower of this age was short-lived, spoilt by autumn

Pl. 46

Pl. 47

[28]

almost before it was open. And as the artists at work in the potteries of ancient Athens were uninspired in the age when contemporary sculptors were decorating the Parthenon, we cannot feel that by the art of illumination, which in the fifteenth century has become a minor art in England, master hands were attracted. *Si quis amat, non laborat* is part of the motto of a workshop from which some fine books of the period come. And in the best the workmanship still looks like a labour of love. But in the majority it is unexciting and may be commonplace or vulgar. There is little material to judge whether there were great painters working on a larger scale. If much else was produced of the quality of the *Wilton Diptych* or the Virgin of the Winchester glass, it has been destroyed. In most of *Pls. 46, 47* the good books there is brilliant colour, minute detail and lively incident and a sense of what can be done in a small space. But the work of most is unambitious and the charm of many fortuitous. By the mid-fifteenth century Englishmen with money and with pretentions to taste travelled abroad frequently. Like all good Englishmen with money and with pretentions to taste always, they thought that what they bought abroad must be better than what was made in England. This time, they were right.

Notes

(i) The picture to which reference is made is the Brueghel *Icarus*.

(ii) Here I had in mind the Dürer engraving of *St. Jerome*.

(iii) For details, see Millar, *The Lindisfarne Gospels,* introduction, p. 11

(iv) The 'undoubtedly English' work is that in the Northumbrian books; and I consider also that *Amiatinus*, f. 796. v, is probably by a native artist working in the classical tradition. As compared with the *St. Augustine Gospels* from Corpus Christi College, Cambridge, this is crude and unsophisticated, though the original the artist had before him must have been very close in style to the pictures in the Corpus book.

(v) Cf. Masai, *Les origines de la Miniature dite Irlandaise,* pl. XLIX-LVII. These parallels are amongst the most valuable features of M. Masai's book.

(vi) Mr. Tolhurst believes that the *Benedictional of St. Aethelwold* does not come from Winchester but from Ely (cf. *Archaeologia,* LXXXIII). There are difficulties in his argument. He claims that the *chorus virginum* is represented by two full pages among the preliminaries, but that the *chorus martyrum* has only one; a fact which he rightly argues would indicate association with a monastery dedicated to a female saint. But his fact is wrong. That there were originally two pages of martyrs is proved by the inscription. The existing page has *martyrum* of the two words *chorus martyrum*, the inscription on the two pages of virgins being similarly spaced out. He has however rightly shown that Winchester was not the original centre of Aethelwold's reforms, but Abingdon; and that books have been recklessly attributed to Winchester on the grounds of the so-called Winchester style. But the New Minster *Edgar Charter,* the *Liber Vitae,* the little book of miscellanies with drawings by the same artist as the *Liber Vitae* and its tiny companion volume, and the *Grimbald Gospels,* are all certainties for Winchester, as is at the end of the period *B. M. Arundel 60.* I am inclined personally to add the *Benedictional of St. Aethelwold.* But with or without that, in terms of quantity but specially of quality, the list is impressive.

(vii) *British Museum Cotton MS. Nero C iv*, from which our Pl. 5 (not one of the illuminations in question here) is taken.

(viii) e.g. the Tournai font; the British Museum has an enamel half roundel on which Henry of Blois is represented. It is considered French.

(ix) I have in mind the *Missal of Nicholas Lytlington* in Westminster Abbey Library. The *gorgoneion* might be copied from a jewel, but something suspiciously like it appears already in twelfth century Romanesque sculpture.

NOTES

(x) The factors I have in mind as accounting for the prosperity of the Norwich area are the reconciliation with the King after a disturbed period in 1286, and the growth of the wool trade. Up to the last years of the thirteenth century there is we are told 'little reason to suppose that Norwich derived much wealth from the wool trade . . . the *lanator* or wool merchant is seldom met with in our earliest records. . . . On the other hand the Cistercian abbeys of Sibton, Garendon, Combe, and Woburn held property along the river bank of Conesford, presumably for the convenience of shipping the wool on their Norfolk estates, while four others of the same order had property in Norwich'. The wool staple was removed from Norwich in 1357 and was permanently fixed in Calais in 1376. The period 1290-1360 appears to be that of the great East Anglian books. The Black Death may have had an effect on the decline of the area.

(xi) *The Sherborne Missal:* Millar, *English Illuminated Manuscripts,* II, Frontispiece and Pls. 83, 84.

(xii) This point was worked out in my *Artists of the Winchester Bible,* especially pp. 13, 14.

APPENDIX I

The Book of Durrow and the Northumbrian Style

This copy of the Gospels has traditional associations with Ireland, and is now in the library of Trinity College, Dublin. It is generally agreed to be the earliest known book in the style here called Northumbrian (often called Hiberno-Saxon) and the question of its origin is therefore of special interest. Since there were Irish and English working side by side in the Northumbrian monasteries, a fact which we know not only from Bede but from books that show English and Irish hands working in the same volume, the question is a complex one. Points which have a bearing on it are here set down in summary form.

(i) The old assumption that this style was Irish in origin was natural in view of the quantity of later medieval work, indubitably Irish, executed in it. Irish work of the twelfth century was still using these formulae when they had disappeared from English work three and a half centuries before. The style seemed, to antiquaries fifty years ago, to be peculiarly Irish in origin because it was peculiarly Irish in later medieval times.

(ii) The *Book of Durrow* has a note, or 'colophon', written in the first person, saying that it was copied by Columba, in twelve days. St. Columba (died *c.* 597) was founder of the monastery of Durrow in Ireland, where the book was later kept. There are many difficulties about this colophon. Some of the material passages have at some time been erased and re-written, among them that containing Columba's name, and this has caused the genuineness of the colophon as a whole to be suspect. Moreover, a chemical re-agent has at some time been used to decipher what were the original words under the erasure, and this makes it even harder now to ascertain the facts. Its appearance now, however, suggests that the re-written letters follow the lines of the original inscription; as if, after an attempt had been made for some reason to erase them, they had been re-written in their original form.

If this is so (and why it should be so is certainly a puzzle), that would seem at first sight to be conclusive of the book's Irish origin. It does not follow. There are in existence a few fragments of writing which may be actually in Columba's own hand. (See Lowe, *Codices Latini Antiquiores* Pt. II no. 266, with plate.) It is a much earlier hand than that of the colophon or of the *Book of Durrow* as a whole. If the colophon is not a late addition but contemporary with the book, as it may be, this is only one of many instances where the scribe copied out, not only the book before him, but also

[32]

its colophon as he found it. We need go no further than *Codex Epternacensis,* a book which belongs approximately to the same generation as *Durrow,* for a certain example of this. A colophon in that book, copied doubtless from its exemplar, dates it 558 and connects it with a Neapolitan abbot. Actually its date is at least a century and a quarter later and there is good reason for thinking that it belonged to St. Willibrord and was made in his day. *Durrow* cannot be of St. Columba's date; and if it is only a *copy* of a book written in Columba's hand, that leaves the place of *Durrow's* own origin undetermined.

Pls. 52c, 53a

(iii) There is the powerful authority of Professor E. A. Lowe (*Codices Latini Antiquiores,* Part II, no. 273) for the view that the hands in which *Durrow* as a whole is written are Northumbrian. Professor Lowe has no doubts about this. It is one of the instances in which he thinks that a distinction between an Irish and a Northumbrian hand can certainly be drawn.

(iv) His view is strongly supported as he points out (following Burkitt) by the character of the text. At this early date the Latin version of the Bible was not yet as fully standardized as it later became. There were considerable verbal differences between the Latin text of the Gospels current in Ireland and that used in Northumbria. The text of *Durrow* is Northumbrian in character.

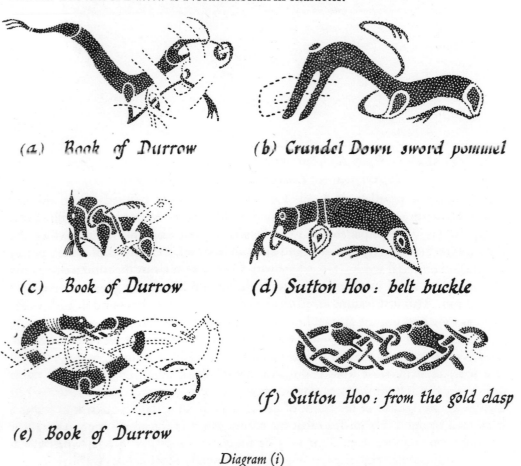

(a) *Book of Durrow*

(b) *Crundel Down sword pommel*

(c) *Book of Durrow*

(d) *Sutton Hoo : belt buckle*

(f) *Sutton Hoo : from the gold clasp*

(e) *Book of Durrow*

Diagram (i)
b, c, d, after the British Museum Provisional Guide (Bruce Mitford)

(v) The Irish calligraphic tradition, so far as we know anything of it before the date of *Durrow*, is uninspired. For an Irish majuscule hand probably earlier than *Durrow* cf. Lowe *C.L.A.* no. 441 (from Bobbio); cf. also no. 271. Most Irish books of the *Durrow* period are in minuscule hands, and have few calligraphic pretensions. The best of the books produced in English monasteries during the seventh century in uncial hands based on continental models, are calligraphically very fine. The hand ultimately to be developed from the fusion of the two contains Irish elements. But the English parent is perhaps equally important, for it is certainly this that sets the high artistic standard. We need not be surprised therefore if the same turns out to be true of the decoration.

(vi) The great discovery made in 1938 of Anglo-Saxon treasure at Sutton Hoo, treasure buried perhaps a decade before *Durrow* was written, has brought about a revaluation of Anglo-Saxon art at this period. That treasure contains not only work of superlatively fine quality, showing all the main types of motif seen in the *Durrow* decoration, (excepting of course the specifically Christian Evangelist symbols), but

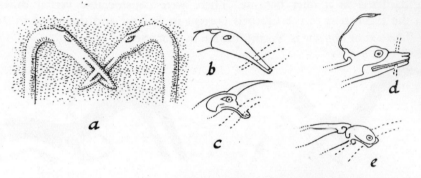

Diagram (ii)
(a) Monkwearmouth Sculpture; after Hodgkin, History of the Anglo-Saxons,
(b) Durrow, (c) Lindisfarne, (d) St. Chad, (e) Kells

also remarkable parallels of detail. One of these, already pointed out in the first British Museum publication of the treasure by Mr. Bruce Mitford, is here illustrated (Diagram (i)) for comparison. As can be seen in that diagram, features which the Sutton Hoo animals ((i) d. and f.) and animals from other examples of contemporary Anglo-Saxon metal work ((i) b.) share with *Durrow* animals are the curious elongation of the snout, and the treatment of the joint almost as if it were designed to swivel on a central pin. This first feature, in particular, does not seem to be found in Irish work. And as time goes on, the animal heads from the interlaced designs grow blunter, and the features more naturalistic,—as a result, no doubt of the influence of the 'classical' models from Italy—so that for a close parallel to the *Durrow* animals, we have to look at a sculptured interlace from Monkwearmouth, dated about 675 ((ii) a, b) rather than at the heads from the later interlace pages of *Lindisfarne, St. Chad,* or *Kells*. Where there is an elongation of the snout of the animals in those later books, it becomes a beak on a recognizable bird, so that the requirements of the artist's more naturalistic demands can thus be met. This may be found in *Lindisfarne, passim,* where it has indeed been claimed that the species of bird is actually identifiable. We may stop far short of that claim, and yet maintain that there is some naturalism about them.

Diagram (ii),
c–e

(vii) An obvious detail which connects *Echternach* and the *Kalendar and Martyrology of Willibrord* with *Durrow*, and which, if a fourth book, the Durham MS. *A II 7*, were complete, we might have found in it also,* is a vertical space filler, to be seen in Diagram (iii). In *Durrow* and in the *Kalendar of Willibrord,* the form this takes is almost indistinguishable; (cf. *Lowe,* II Plate facing p. xiii, with Pl. 273, right hand; our (iii) c) and in *Echternach* it is a development at one remove only from the original ((iii) d.). Most important of all, we have the common use of certain artistic devices to be seen most clearly in the smaller initials; the eccentric 'wire' spiral, the small drop-shaped ornament at the point of an initial, the reservation of tiny rounds of white within the heavy black lines of an initial, the tiny white circle itself sometimes containing a dot; all these connect the group and link it with *Lindisfarne*. By the time that *Lindisfarne* is produced, however, a new set of artistic ideas and standards are developing.

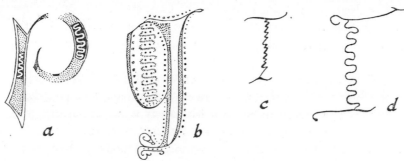

Diagram (iii)
(a) Durrow, (b) Cathach of St. Columba, (c) Durrow and the Calendar
of St. Willibrord, (d) Echternach

For that reason I am not prepared to claim that *Lindisfarne* comes certainly from the same atelier. It might possibly represent the work of another Northumbrian monastery.

(viii) *Durrow* is stylistically the earliest of this group of four related books. If the others are Northumbrian, *Durrow* will also be Northumbrian, not Irish. But Lowe regards the *Echternach Gospels* and the *Martyrology* as the points of certainty from which a study of the Northumbrian hands must begin. The Evangelist Symbol for Matthew, in the *Echternach Gospels*, is tonsured. As is well known, the method of tonsure was a matter for intense controversy in the eighth century, and there was a violent division of opinion between the Anglo-Saxons who had adopted the Roman tonsure and the Irish who maintained their own (apparently pre-Christian) pattern. We do not know certainly what this Irish pattern was.† What we do know for certain, however, is that the *Echternach* figure has the Roman tonsure. He has been undoubtedly given it on purpose; and this detail stamps the book decisively as Anglo-Saxon. The relationships between *Echternach, Durrow* and *Durham* are difficult to determine precisely. In particular it is difficult to discover in the drawing of the human figure and its draperies any significant connexions between them (see Appendix II). But the ornament in the initial letters of the text forms an unmistakable series, with *Durrow*

Pl. 53a

* This was written on the basis of notes made many years ago (when I was not looking for this particular feature) and photographs necessarily incomplete. I have recently re-examined the book and excellent examples of this vertical space filler actually occur, in the genealogy in *Luke*. They are very close to the Echternach example.

† It is described as being 'from ear to ear'. The *Echternach* tonsure is certainly not that, whatever the phrase may mean. For a later representation of this Roman tonsure, cf. St. Peter in Pl. 4.

as the earliest of the three, using no animal forms in its initial decoration and virtually no interlacing within the stems of the initials themselves, only a filling, curled like the gut of an animal, inside the initial's stem (cf. Diagram (iii) a), *Echternach*, using still no animal forms in this initial decoration, but filling the stems of the initials with geometric interlace in addition to the 'gut' filling; and *Durham* using animal forms freely (as well as the gut filling), including their use in the filling of the stems. These three books are connected in addition to points mentioned above in (vii), by the similarity of script used in them, and by the use of a particular form of filling for line endings (*ssssssss* or continuously *ᴧᴧᴧᴧᴧ* —it is found in both varieties as early as *Durrow*) which they share, and a variant of which is found in *Durham A. II 16*, also doubtless a Northumbrian book. And the first page of *Echternach* seems to be actually written in the same hand as part of *Durham* (e.g. the leaf illustrated by Lowe, no. 149). The *Martyrology* is not a copy of the Gospels like the other three. It is not therefore comparable with them in that it has no elaborate initials. But it is certainly next of kin to them. Incidentally the same line ending occurs, but only twice, in *Lindisfarne*.

It is worth noting that the subsequent history of this *SSS* filling, which appears in *Kells* in the form *ᴄᴧᴧᴧᴧᴄ* (cf. also Lowe Pl. 217) would be consistent with the view that *Kells* was produced in an Irish Monastery where the artistic tradition had been strongly influenced by men who had worked in Northumbria. (In *C.C.C. Camb. no. 144*, a still later variant of it occurs, in a book perhaps copied in the south from a Northumbrian exemplar.)

(ix) In view of all this, there seems to be no reasonable doubt that *Durrow* was produced in Northumbria, and was copied from an exemplar in the hand of St. Columba, which had been extensively corrected to bring it into conformity with the Northumbrian text. And in my opinion there is little doubt that the 'Hiberno-Saxon' style of which *Durrow* is such a fine example, was, primarily, Northumbrian in origin. The interlaced animal pattern was derived from the work of Anglo-Saxon craftsmen, particularly metal workers. The date of the *Lindisfarne Gospels* is about 700. It is datable with certainty within a generation. That of *Durrow* should be at least a quarter of a century earlier. The text of *Durrow* makes it certain that it is later than the arrival of Theodore in 664 from Italy. The design makes it certain that it is very little later.

(x) If we had Irish books of the period between the date of St. Columba and the *Book of Durrow*, we might be able to recognize certain details in *Durrow* as having an Irish rather than an Anglo-Saxon ancestry. One of the initials in the Columba fragments to which reference is made in (ii) above, an initial in the fragment illustrated in Lowe, *op. cit.*, has a filling that might conceivably be the ancestor of the 'gut' filling. Cf. Diagram (iii) above. And at the top right hand corner appears to be a tiny open loop such as is frequent in the smaller capital initials of the early Northumbrian books. Another initial ends in a tiny animal's head. And as it has recently been pointed out these fragments suggest that the habit of setting the initial letter within the frame of the written surface of the page, instead of outside, in the margin, may have been learned by the scribe of *Durrow* from an Irish source. It was not usual elsewhere. It would be absurd to exclude the likelihood of Irish influence. Nothing could be more likely. But Irish influence does not mean Irish origin.

cf. below, p. 41

APPENDIX I

(xi) It is however debatable whether the question 'Anglo-Saxon or Irish' is a proper question. As has been mentioned above we know from contemporary documents that Anglo-Saxon and Irish monks lived and worked side by side, in the Northumbrian monasteries. We have books in which the text is written in two hands, one of the two having a clearly Irish, the other clearly Anglo-Saxon, character. (A parallel exists in the Tours books of the late eighth century, after Alcuin had gone from York to Tours. There are at least two Tours books of this time in which part of the text is in an Anglo-Saxon, part in a continental hand.) We have books in which the text of one Gospel belongs to the English tradition, another to the Irish tradition. In Northumbria these two traditions met, and however much, or however little, the Irish tradition contributed to Northumbrian artistic achievement, our sources show beyond doubt that its contribution to Northumbrian learning was of high importance. And when the artist of the figures in the *Lindisfarne Gospels* adds their names in Greek, the addition is not because he was copying a Byzantine model, but because the ostentatious use of Greek tags was characteristic of Irish learning. Little Greek was generally understood. The Greek scholarship of Erigena belongs to a later period. But what there was was made to go a very long way, and it was this which led the scribe of *Echternach* to write ΦINIT instead of FINIT and the artist of the *Lindisfarne* Evangelists to write O AGIOS instead of SANCTUS.* Irish influence in scholarship—and also in ascetic practice—was powerful in Northumbria. But in matters of art it was far less significant. The main stream flows in the reverse direction, from Monkwearmouth and Lindisfarne to Kells.

* Note that the name is not Greek in form (IOHANNES)—a point that will illustrate the sketchiness of the Artist's Greek. Similarly, he spells Luke with a Latin 'c', not with a Greek 'k'.

APPENDIX II

The Representation of the Human Figure in Northumbrian Manuscripts, and in Manuscripts produced in the South, 675–825

As yet no satisfactory parallels can be adduced to suggest the origins of the extraordinary styles of figure drawing that developed in the north in the seventh, eighth and ninth centuries. The history of figure drawing in the south of England is comparatively clear. It is a classical revival. If we compare the imitation with late classical works which are its originals or similar to them the imitation is stronger, if cruder, than they. At first the figure style is clumsy but painstaking, like that of the Psalter from Canterbury. The script of this is a fine uncial, apparently unaffected by any Irish influence. The famous page which shows King David and his orchestra has Anglo-Saxon (so called Celtic) motifs in the decoration, fine trumpet spirals, fret pattern and so forth, interspersed with Frankish and classical ornaments; but the figures (like the script) are untouched by 'Irish' influence and aspire to be classical; as do the Evangelists of *Codex Aureus* in Stockholm, one of which is here illustrated side by side with the David. The fall of the drapery from the knees in these two is so closely similar that the two designs may well actually be by the same hand. Another classical figure is the Evangelist St. Matthew from the *Rome Gospels*, and in places in this book (e.g. in the great monogram page illustrated in Kendrick, *Anglo-Saxon Art*, Pl. LVI) we seem to have represented what is here also an essentially uncial script, though here the script of the text as a whole is no longer pure uncial.

These rather heavy classical imitations in the south are transformed about the end of the eighth century. In the *Canterbury Gospels*, the period of which is Carolingian, we have Evangelists which belong in their essentials to the later Anglo-Saxon style. It would be natural to date the St. Mark into the tenth or eleventh centuries did not the ornaments of the roundel suggest an earlier period, and this early date is confirmed by the opening page of St. Luke. The Evangelist in the roundel at the top of this page represents again unmistakably the later Anglo-Saxon style, but the ornament of the page as a whole is equally unmistakable as eighth/ninth century. We must therefore take seriously the suggestion that the brilliant, sketchy style which comes into Western European art at about A.D. 800 was practised in England as early as it was on the continent. It is by no means impossible that it originated in

Pl. 53, b-d

Pl. 53c

Pl. 53d

Pl. 54c

England, for the reputation of English books in Charlemagne's own view clearly stood high. No one questions that the Anglo-Saxon script had a wide influence on the continent. It is thus a possibility that the 'one artist of genius' with whom as is suggested in the text the style must have begun, worked at first in England. *cf. above, p. 13*

The outlines of this part of the story are reasonably clear. When we come to the Northumbrian books, it is a very different matter. The series of Evangelists in these books and in those related to them has no single common factor. The Evangelist Matthew, in *Durrow*, is an Anglo-Saxon metal-work figure. The inlays and enamels provide close parallels to his elaborate chequered cloak, which does not pretend to be drapery. A sort of parallel to his spreading bobbed hair can perhaps be traced on the Sutton Hoo helmet; the stylization of his face bears no close resemblance to the stylized faces of later Northumbrian books and may be original. He is *sui generis*. As soon as we advance a few years to the time of *Echternach*, however, an extraordinary change has taken place. Here the drapery has assumed the elaborate rolls that are characteristic *Pl. 53a* of later figures, though here they are more carefully formalized and patterned with a far minuter detail than in the later books. The nearest thing to the *Echternach* St. Matthew is the *Chad* St. Luke, where the loops of drapery are formalized in the same way, and where there is something of the same precision in the drawing of feet and hands, though the quality is not so fine and the pattern nothing like so meticulous. In the *Chad* St. Mark the drapery is closer, though certainly not really similar, to the Durham Crucifixion, and the treatment of the hair is utterly different in the two pictures. Later developments of this extraordinary formalization in drapery are the Crucifixion in the Irish Psalter at St. John's College, Cambridge, the Evangelists in the *MacRegol Gospels* and the drapery on the crucified figure in *St. Gall, MS. 51*.

But these are offshoots, and the main development does not take this form. It is strongly affected immediately after the production of the *Durham Gospels* by the introduction of classical models, used by the artist of the *Lindisfarne Gospels*. One of these models is known (cf. Millar, *Lindisfarne Gospels*, Pl. XXXVII). Familiarity with them makes the artist of the *Lindisfarne Gospels* produce considerably more naturalistic figures than his predecessors had done, though there is of course nothing in them that gives the sense of natural fall such as is given by the classical draperies of his model. Nevertheless compared for instance with *Echternach*, naturalistic they are. In this, and in several other respects,—such a decorative detail for instance as the double sided view of an animal's head from above, which is used again and again in *Kells*, appears sparsely already in *Lindisfarne*,—the line that leads to the *Book of Kells* seems to lead through the *Lindisfarne Gospels*; for while the faces in *Kells* are so strongly formalized, the clothes, if formalized, are nevertheless distinguishable as clothes (cf. *Kells ff.* 7v, 28v, 29v, etc.); which is more than can be said of the *Echternach* or *Chad* draperies. The line from *Kells* leads eventually to the *MacDurnan Gospels* now at Lambeth, where the undergarment of the St. Matthew, under that incredibly voluminous cloak, must have been copied from something like the skirt of the Virgin in *Kells*. 7v.

The seated David in the Durham *Cassiodorus* is a near relative to the *Lindisfarne* figures. The artist of the David seems to have had no classical models to copy direct, only a model similar to the *Lindisfarne* St. John. With this his work has various

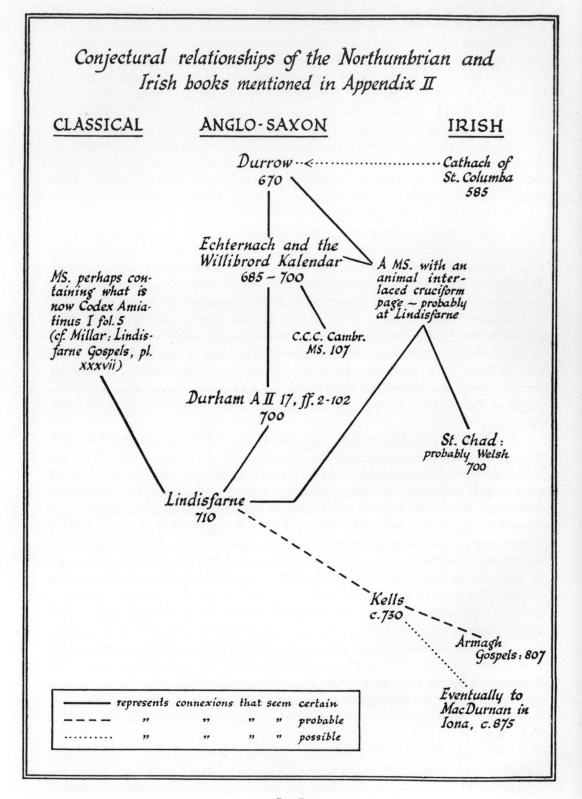

Conjectural relationships of the Northumbrian and
Irish books mentioned in Appendix II

CLASSICAL   ANGLO-SAXON   IRISH

Durrow···<·············Cathach of
670   St. Columba
                          585

Echternach and the
Willibrord Kalendar   A MS. with an
685 – 700   animal inter-
                   laced cruciform

MS. perhaps con-   page – probably
taining what is   at Lindisfarne
now Codex Amia-
tinus I fol. 5
(cf. Millar: Lindis-   C.C.C. Cambr.
farne Gospels, pl.   MS. 107
XXXvii)

Durham A II 17, ff. 2-102
700

                              St. Chad :
                          probably Welsh
                          700

Lindisfarne
710

                          Kells
                          c.730
                                Armagh
                                Gospels : 807

                                Eventually to
                                MacDurnan in
                                Iona, c.875

———— represents connexions that seem certain
– – – –   ”   ”   ”   ”   probable
··········   ”   ”   ”   ”   possible

similarities—such as the thick folds over the shoulder, the decoration at the neck and the treatment of the hair.

Thus we seem to be able to trace several lines of development in the figure drawing. The first is the classical development in the south, which grows into the rapid impressionistic style of the Carolingian renaissance. The second has as its only existing representative the *Durrow* Evangelist. This is a purely Anglo-Saxon style. The third style of figure drawing begins for us with *Echternach*, continues through *Chad* and branches out on the one hand into the debased 'Irish' books (which may indeed be Irish) like the *MacRegol* and the *St. Gall Gospels*, and on the other, through *Lindisfarne* with its strong classical influence in the figure drawing, back to Ireland and Iona in *Kells* and *MacDurnan*; while in Northumbria itself, so far as our extant examples suggest, it comes to an end with the Durham *Cassiodorus*.

It may be useful to set out the following points about the origin and date of *Kells*, and its connexion with earlier Irish work:

(*a*) M. Masai holds the view that there are no Irish books of fine workmanship, and therefore questions whether *Kells* can have been made in Ireland. He includes a miniature plate of the *Armagh Gospels*, which can be dated certainly and localized certainly, the date being 807 and the provenance Armagh. Even M. Masai's plate suggests the excellence of the workmanship of this book. It is in fact brilliant, and the fierce precision of the opening with the Evangelist symbols is as good as it could be. The book is not on a grand scale. But its quality is superb. There can be no justification, then, in the denial of our Irish origin for *Kells* on the grounds that Irish scribes were incapable of precise workmanship.

(*b*) In addition to the series illustrated in our diagram (ii), the following points are worth noting: (1) Kendrick's Sequence of the Great Monogram pages, suggesting a date for *Kells* after *Lindisfarne*; (2) *Durrow* with no animal ornament in the initials; animal ornament appears very rarely in *Echternach*; frequently in *Durham* and *Lindisfarne*, though as yet no human interlace designs are used; human designs frequently used in *Kells*, with exceptionally elaborate animal ornament also; (3) The *Vitulus* symbol on f. 290*b* of *Kells* fits into the sequence, *Echternach*, unwinged, with the joints marked by strange enamel technique curves, the outline being still very close to *Durrow*; *Kells*, joints similarly marked, but *vitulus* winged; *Armagh Gospels, vitulus* winged with vestiges of the marks at the joints.

Pl. 52c
Pl. 52d

For Irish work of the sixth and seventh centuries, we have to go back to the *Cathach of St. Columba*, datable Irish books from Bobbio, and the *Bangor Antiphonary*. These show that the practice of following a large initial with letters of gradually decreasing size is Irish (this, pointed out to me by Mr. Wormald as an Irish feature, is conspicuously copied in Northumbrian work, but does not occur in *St. Chad*); that the practice of splitting the stem of an initial for decorative purposes is Irish [*Cathach of St. Columba*, cf. also *Lowe* 350, from Bobbio, early seventh century]; that the reserved circle with dot is Irish [*Bangor Antiphonary*]; and most important of all, that already before the end of the sixth century an Irish scribe could end an initial in an animal's head [*Cathach of St. Columba*]. These points give us good indications of the extent of Irish influence.

List of Plates in Chronological Order

PLATES 2 (*facing page 8*), 9, 10   *The Book of Durrow c. 670*
Trinity College, Dublin, MS. A. iv 5

The question of the origin of the copy of the gospels is fully discussed in Appendix I. We do not know how or when it reached Ireland, but it has been in Ireland for all its recorded history, and might even have been taken back by Colman in 664. If so, it was at that time a new book, for it cannot be more than a few years earlier than that date. Some of it is now in a tattered state, as one of our plates shows (Pl. 10*b*) and it is surprising that the book has survived at all, since it is said that water used to be poured over it in order that ailing cattle might be treated with the magic liquid. There is at present only one 'animal folio', only one page in which interlaced animals are part of an elaborate pattern (Pl. 9*b*), and it was doubtless another book, somewhat later, with a cruciform animal page that was the common ancestor of *Lindisfarne* and *Chad* (Pls. 12, 13 and 14). The other existing pattern pages have no animal forms. The *vitulus* of St. Luke is very close to the *Echternach vitulus* (Pl. 52c, d), while the Lion of St. Mark (Pl. 2) has a splendid 'all the better to eat you with' look about him. The pattern pages (examples are Pls. 9, 10) are still magnificent; many parallels for the trumpet spiral pattern of Pl. 10*b* can be seen on the hanging bowls from Anglo-Saxon graves. Pl. 2 gives a good idea of the colours used by the illuminator.

PLATES 11, 52c, 53a *The Echternach Gospels. Seventh Century. Fourth Quarter*
Now Paris Bibliothèque Nationale, Lat. 9389

This wonderful book is associated with the monastery founded by St. Willibrord (cf. p. 12) in Germany, and there is good reason to suppose that he took it with him from Northumbria. Its close association with other Northumbrian books is discussed in Appendix I, sections vii and viii. Its present condition is one of extraordinary freshness. Our illustrations show (Pl. 11) the superb lion of St. Mark rampant across the page, the heifer of St. Luke (Pl. 52c) so close to the *Durrow* heifer, and 53a the strange *imago hominis* of St. Matthew, discussed on p. 35. The border of Pl. 53a should be compared with the *Durrow* border in Pl. 52a. Pl 11 may give the impression that the book was unfinished. I do not think that this is so. The reserved spaces are a calculated part of a fine design.

[42]

PLATES 12 and 13   *The St. Chad Gospels c. 700*
                                               Now Lichfield Cathedral Library

The Cruciform animal folio, illustrated in Pls. 12 and 13, doubtless approximately contemporary with that illustrated in Pl. 14, must have a common ancestor with that, for nothing else in this book suggests direct descent from *Lindisfarne*. There are early notes in Welsh in the book. It bears none of the characteristic traces of Irish *see p. 41, b* books, and it may perhaps have been made in Wales under strong Northumbrian influence. The tradition of its connexion with St. Chad cannot be sustained after analysis of its style and contents. This book was made after the date of Chad's death. But it is by no means impossible that its text and some of its ornament was copied from a Gospel book which bore St. Chad's name rightly (as the *Book of Durrow* was copied from one bearing St. Columba's name) and that when this book was complete, therefore, (it now has many pages missing) it had an inscription connecting it with St. Chad as *Durrow's* inscription connects it with St. Columba. There is no reasonable doubt that the original of the cruciform page came from Northumbria, from which Chad himself came.

PLATES 14 and 15   *The Lindisfarne Gospels c. 700*
                                  Now British Museum, Cotton MS. Nero, D vi

The condition of the book is still fresh. Its pages are hardly stained, in spite of the tradition of its immersion, early in its history, in the sea. It contains a long note—not contemporary, but nevertheless early, the information in which there is no reason for rejecting—which gives an account of its origin (cf. p. 22). The liveliness of its animal forms as used in the great cruciform animal folio (Pl. 14) is unsurpassed perhaps by any comparable forms anywhere. The grave and dignified drawings of the evangelists (Pl. 15) are discussed on p. 39. The most important of its pages are magnificently illustrated, and questions of origin and design fully discussed in E. G. Millar, *The Lindisfarne Gospels*, pp. 1-8. It may be claimed that, while the decoration of the *Book of Kells* (not included in this series of plates, since it must clearly be regarded as an Irish book) now in the Library of Trinity College, Dublin, is more complex and elaborate, the taste and restraint of the *Lindisfarne Gospels* make it without rival.

PLATE 3   *The Benedictional of St. Aethelwold c. 975. Probably Winchester*
(*facing page* 14)   *In the library of the Duke of Devonshire*

An inscription in this book, giving some details of its making, is discussed on p. 22. Our plate shows the ascent of Christ into Heaven; there is a background of tempestuous skies and angels which seems almost to prefigure a Last Judgment and which is in harmony with the solemn severity of the figure. The *Benedictional* has a whole series of illuminated pages with figure subjects and is undoubtedly the most important monument of later Anglo-Saxon illumination. Only one is illustrated here, because it is one of those books for which reproduction in colour is essential if we are to get any impression of the artist's intention.

[43]

PLATES 17, 18, 19   *The Grimbald Gospels c. 1020 Probably Winchester*
Now British Museum, Add. MS. 34890

This book gets its name from its containing a copy of a letter commending Grimbald (who was associated with the early history of the 'New Minster' at Winchester) to King Alfred. It is this letter which makes the association of the book with Winchester probable. The details here illustrated are the *Evangelist Luke* (Pl. 17) and part of the two borders which, in the manuscript itself, face one another, at the opening of the Gospel of St. John. Manuscripts of the so-called Winchester School (cf. p. 30, note *iv*) have as one of their characteristics an elaborate frame to the decorated page, such as is seen in Pl. 3. Usually these frames are filled with foliage. In this book the artist has, with brilliant effect, filled the upper parts of the frame, illustrated, with angels. The drawing is of great delicacy. In the three roundels of Pl. 18 are the Three Persons of the Trinity. In the centre roundel of Pl. 19 is a Virgin and Child, one of the earliest representations in an existing English book of this theme; flanked, in the roundel on either side, by the seraphim. The drawing of the angels' wings and feet should be compared with the Winchester Anglo-Saxon Ivory (cf. Kendrick, *Late Saxon and Viking Art,* Pl. xxxviii, 3).

PLATE 16   *The York Anglo-Saxon Gospels c. 1000*
Minster Library, York

The Evangelist Mark; one of the three evangelist pages remaining in this Gospel book. The 'Winchester' type of work is conspicuous by its absence from the frames of these pages, but characteristic foliage of the type appears at some of the knots of the initials. My impression is that this book was made just after the turn of the century rather than before it. Its place of origin is unknown, but it is not improbable that it was made in the north of England, though the spirit of the drawing is so close to that of the *Grimbald Gospels.*

PLATES 20, 21   *Psalter c. 1020. Probably from Bury St. Edmunds*
Now in the Vatican Library, MS. Reg. Lat. 12

Pl. 20 shows a marginal drawing of the Ascension. As so often in medieval representations of this theme, the subject is indicated by the feet of the ascending figure only, at the top of the picture. On either side are angels pointing towards the ascending figure, and the rest of the margin is decorated with sketches of the disciples, sketches in which their astonishment and the suddenness of the event is brilliantly indicated. The two figures below that of the Angel, in the left margin, represent the Virgin and St. John.

Pl. 21 shows three details from other parts of the book. (*a*) shows an angel conveying the soul to Abraham's bosom, and here again the representation of rushing movement is very effective. The other details show a king at prayer and the wheel of Psalm 83, v. 13.

PLATES 4 (*facing page 16*), 22 *The New Minster Liber Vitae c. 1020. Winchester*

Now British Museum, MS. Stowe 944

The drawings are in a brown ink, heightened with colour in a way of which Pl. 4 gives a good impression. That plate shows King Canute and Queen Aelfgyfu presenting a Gold Cross to the New Minster at Winchester; above in a mandorla flanked by figures of the Virgin and St. Peter (patron saint of the monastery) is the beardless figure of Christ. Below are monks of the New Minster. The other plate from this book (Pl. 22) is described in the text, following the description in Millar, *English Illuminated MSS. of the Tenth to Thirteenth Centuries*, pp. 19, 20. The artist, who is certainly the artist of the drawings in another British Museum manuscript (*Cotton MS. Titus D. XXVII*, cf. also *Titus D. XXVI*) was apparently named Aelfwine.

PLATE 24 *New Testament. Probably about 1100 from Bury St. Edmunds*

Now Cambridge, Pembroke College, MS. 120

In this book the text is preceded by a great series of coloured drawings (from which our details are taken), earlier than the book itself and perhaps done about 1100. The effect of the fresh colours is evidently a most important part of the artist's purpose in the original, but is singularly difficult to reproduce, and after repeated attempts at colour reproduction had been made, the blocks were rejected. The details reproduced show (*a*) the miraculous Draught of fishes, (*b*) the Entombment, and give some idea of the solemn dignity which is characteristic of this artist's work.

PLATE 5 *The St. Swithun Psalter c. 1140 Winchester (The Old Minster)*
(*facing page* 18) *Now British Museum, MS. Cotton, Nero C. vi*

The shepherds and the Angels; one of a series of coloured drawings preceding the psalter. As can be seen in the reproduction, the background has apparently been scraped for the sake of the *lapis lazuli* pigment used on it. The picture remains a magnificent example of the art of its period, so much more powerful than that of the late Anglo-Saxon artists of a century before; and it shows an unusual degree of characterization, the half-witted shepherd, the wise old man, and the youth whose eyes are blinded by a heavenly vision. Many details connect this book very closely with the earliest work in the *Winchester Bible*. The artist named for convenience the *Master of the Leaping Figures* who worked in that book was evidently brought up in the school which produced this psalter, and it is difficult to be certain that one of the hands in it is not his hand at an early stage of development. For these artists, cf. my *Artists of the Winchester Bible*.

PLATE 23 *Wall Painting c. 1160*
Canterbury Cathedral, Chapel of St. Anselm

St. Paul shakes the viper from his hand into the fire. Third quarter of twelfth century; cf. Tristram, *Medieval English Wall Painting, the Twelfth Century*; p. 105, and plates. Our plate is photographed from the original.

PLATES 25 to 28 *The Winchester Bible c. 1150-70. Winchester, the Old Minster*
Still in the library of Winchester Cathedral

The plates all illustrate work designed in the earlier period of work on the *Bible,* though in Pls. 25 (*b*) and 26 the finish is due, as so often in this book, to a different and stylistically later hand. The two drawings are the work of an artist named for convenience the *Master of the Apocrypha drawings.* Both Pls. 27 and 28 come from the same page of drawings which is, in the original, in three tiers, and is one of two full pages in the same hand illustrating scenes from the Apocrypha. Our reproductions (considerably reduced) show the battle of Samaria (cf. I Maccabees, vii; the arm and head hung up outside the city are those of Nicanor; cf. verse 4) the death of Judas Maccabeus, and the entombment of Judas Maccabeus. Attention may be drawn especially to the tremendous power of the latter group, and the symbolism of the cloak swept upwards to indicate violent emotion. If it were safe to argue from another book (at one time during the twelfth century at St. Albans) in which this master's handiwork—or that of an artist most intimately associated with him—can be seen, we could say that these drawings were intended not to be painted but to be picked out with a wash of one colour. But I doubt whether this argument is safe, for there are three initials in the *Bible,* fully painted, which are the design of this master. Pl. 56a is from one of them. It shows the Prophet Hosea, side by side with a figure (Pl. 56b, c) from the classical manuscript mentioned above, the copy of Terence in the Bodleian Library at Oxford on which this same master or one of his very close associates worked. See also the note on Pl. 56 (*a*), below.

Pl. 25 shows, side by side, two designs, each by the *Master of the Leaping Figures,* each from the foot of an initial letter. (*b*) shows the young man slaying the Amalekite (the finish, at least of the faces, is in another hand); (*a*) Elisha catching the cloak of Elijah. Pl. 26 shows the famous pair of initial letters that stand at the head of the two versions of the *Psalms.* Two scenes from the Old Testament are represented side by side with two from the New which the Old Testament scenes were considered to prefigure. On the left David is seen rescuing the sheep from bear, and taking a lamb out of the lion's mouth. On the right Christ is seen casting out a Devil (drawn as it leaves the mouth of the sufferer) and (below) the Harrowing of Hell. With Christ is the Archangel. The mouth of Hell is represented as the open jaws of a monster, with eyes and teeth and nostril (cf. p. 3) and into it the Devil, chained, is being thrust down. In the background are rescued souls. These initials to Psalm I, designed evidently by the *Master of the Leaping Figures,* were finished by another hand (the *Master of the Genesis Initial*).

[46]

PLATES 29, 30   *Windows in Canterbury Cathedral c. 1200*

Pl. 30 shows the Patriarch Jared (Genesis v, 15-20). Pl. 29 the Parable of the Sower. (In Pl. 29 the head may perhaps be modern.) These two magnificent designs are both what I should call 'Romanesque' in character. Mr. Herbert Read dates the first as 'Late twelfth century', and calls the other early thirteenth. I certainly cannot question these dates, but in its severity of style the 'Sower' roundel is closer to the books of the Romanesque than to those of the Gothic period. There are good reasons for hesitation before we cross-date between work in two different mediums, and I suspect that the change in style began with the artists working in books.

PLATE 31   *Book of Hours, Sarum Use c. 1240*
Illuminated by W. de Brailes (working in Oxford). Now in the library of C. W. Dyson Perrins, Esq.

This detail is described on p. 20. In our reproduction it is considerably enlarged. The book is a personal, not a ceremonial, copy, forerunner of the innumerable Books of Hours produced in later medieval times for personal use. For the figure with the spear, below, right, cf. Pl. 50.

PLATE 6   *Wall Painting c. 1250*
(*facing page 20*)   *From the Chapel in the Bishop's Palace, Chichester*

This lovely roundel was painted in the mid-thirteenth century. Some metallic paint was used for certain features, and the dark blurs in the reproduction are the censers of the angels, which were evidently painted in silver that has oxidized. It has been reproduced generally from the fine copy made by Professor Tristram, a water-colour now in the Victoria and Albert Museum. The photograph from which this reproduction was made was taken from the original.

PLATES 32, 33   *Apocalypse c. 1290*
Now in the library of C. W. Dyson Perrins, Esq.

The group of Apocalypses, of which this is a fine representative, is sometimes regarded as having been produced at St. Albans, as there is an example—earlier than this—illuminated by Matthew Paris, who worked at St. Albans. By this date, however, monastic production was by no means the rule and we cannot be sure where the books concerned were made (cf. pp. 23, 24). The plates show (32) the writer seeing through the door of heaven (the symbol is constantly used in this series of Apocalypses) the Second Angel sounding the trumpet (Rev. viii, 8); in our reproduction this detail is considerably enlarged; and (33) the Sixth Angel pouring out of his bowl on to the river Euphrates (Rev. xvi, 12)—the writer of the Apocalypse sits near, watching.

PLATES 7 (*facing page 22*) and 34   *The Oscott Psalter. Late thirteenth century*
Now in the library of C. W. Dyson Perrins, Esq.

These two plates are taken from the series of saints which formed the opening pages of the psalter (the origin of which is uncertain; there is no satisfactory clue to show where it was made). It is not possible to determine which saints all the figures were intended to represent. The book in the hand of the saint in Pl. 7 suggests an evangelist. The youthfulness and characteristic pose of the saint in Pl. 34 makes it probable that the subject there is St. John.

PLATE 35   *Single illumination cut out from an Apocalypse c. 1300*

This superb work is normally in the Staatliche Museum, Berlin (*K.I. 672*). I first became aware of it from the photograph in the catalogue of an exhibition held at Wiesbaden in 1946 under the auspices of the Monuments, Fine Arts, and Archives Section of the Office of Military Government. It was there rightly (as I think) described as English, having been previously generally attributed to a German master.

PLATES 1, 8 (*facing page 24*), 36-39
Psalter of Robert de Lisle. Early fourteenth century
Now British Museum, Arundel MS. 83

In its present form, this book consists actually of the fragments of two Psalters, both of approximately the same date, the *Psalter of Robert de Lisle* being much the finer. The magnificent paintings with which this is decorated are among the masterpieces of English illumination. The work of two hands can be readily distinguished in our plates; the artist who works in a more severe tradition and is the greater of the two, is the artist of Pls. 1, 36-39. Pl. 38 shows the Virgin and Child, flanked on either side (lower stage) by saints and (above) by angels. In the sky are two censing angels, whose censers reach into the canopy. The background is of gold, elaborately patterned. Our reproduction is greatly reduced in size, as is that of Pl. 39—a Crucifixion, against an elaborate background of gold and blue. The figure at the foot of the cross is apparently Adam rising from his grave and catching the blood of Christ (for references, see Millar, *English Illuminated MSS., Fourteenth and Fifteenth Centuries*, p. 46). On either side stand the Virgin and the Disciple whom Jesus loved, above are the angels of the sun and moon, and (in the centre) the 'Pelican in her piety' feeding her young with blood by pecking her breast—a frequently used symbol of the Crucifixion. Pl. 37, also much reduced, shows in four compartments the Harrowing of Hell (for an earlier representation cf. note on Pl. 26), the Deposition; the Entombment; and Pilate instructing the soldiers to watch the tomb (cf. Matt. xxvii, 62-65). One of them bears a devil as the charge on his shield. Pl. 1 shows the 'Christ of Pity' (Christ rising from the tomb); the Marys at the tomb; the risen Christ and Mary in the garden; and the risen Christ at meat with two disciples. The feet above symbolize Christ vanishing out of their sight (Luke xxiv. 31). Pl. 36 shows the 'Three living and the three dead', a grim symbol of the vanity of human pleasures. Our reproduction shows this approximately the same size as the original. Pl. 8 shows Christ in Majesty, holding the orb of the world with its triple division (Europe and Africa, divided by the line of the Mediterranean, in the upper half; Asia in the lower half). In the four corners are the evangelists, each with his symbol (cf. pp. 1, 2).

PLATES 40, 41   *The Ormesby Psalter*
Bodleian Library, Oxford, MS. Douce 366

This book gets its name from an early owner, Robert of Ormesby, who gave it to the Cathedral Priory at Norwich. Comment is made in the text (pp. 27, 28) on this book. The details illustrated were probably executed about 1310. The unicorn was believed to lay its head in the lap of a virgin, and thus only could it be captured.

PLATE 42   *The Tickhill Psalter c. 1310*
New York, Public Library

Formerly in the possession of Lord Lothian, this psalter was in the Lothian sale of 1932. The book carries an inscription claiming that John Tickyll *propriis manibus scripsit necnon deauravit*—wrote it with his own hand and gilded it—Tickyll having been Prior of Worksop in the early fourteenth century. In the sale catalogue of the Lothian sale it was assumed that Tickyll was in fact the artist responsible for the decoration. This cannot be the whole truth, for at least three hands are recognizable in the work—in several instances two are recognizable on the same page—a fact which illustrates the danger of relying too far on these inscriptions. The inscription in this instance was written perhaps three generations after the work was done, and while it is likely that John Tickyll paid for the work, or possible as an alternative that he wrote and designed the book himself, the literal interpretation of the inscription is not admissible. The subjects of the four drawings (all in the same hand) in our plate are (*a*) David at the stone Ezel (I Sam. xx, 19, 41); David and Jonathan embrace (I Sam. xx, 41); David sends out spies (I Sam. xxvi, 4); David and Abishai go down into Saul's camp and find him sleeping (I Sam. xxvi, 5-12). They illustrate well the tendency of some fourteenth-century artists to represent almost all their characters simply as charming children (cf. p. 27).

PLATES 43, 44 and 45   *The Queen Mary Psalter. Early fourteenth century*
British Museum, Royal MS. 2. B. VII

Our illustrations show (i) Pl. 43, a complete page of the book showing the layout, with a painting at the top of the page and sketches at the foot, (ii) Pl. 44, full-page tinted drawings—(*a*) a scene from Creation and (*b*) the Quarrel of Hagar and Sarah, and Pl. 45 four decorative details (tinted drawings). The drawings and paintings in this book have been reproduced fully in Warner, *Queen Mary's Psalter*, 1911.

PLATE 46   *The Wilton Diptych. Late fourteenth century*
National Gallery

The question whether this picture is English or French has been hotly discussed. The quality of the work illustrated in the next plate, a work that is English beyond all possible doubt, shows that whatever other grounds may be alleged against the *Wilton Diptych* being English, the excellence of its quality is not in itself sufficient grounds for denying an English origin. The nationality of the artist, however, should perhaps be regarded as still an open question. For the theory of an English origin, cf. Harvey, *Gothic England*, pp. 62-65. The brilliance in the arts of the age of Richard II is discussed on pp. 28, 29, cf. Harvey, *op. cit., passim*. The theory of an English origin is powerfully advocated by Professor E. W. Tristram in *The Month*, June and July 1949.

PLATE 47   *Virgin and Child (glass) 1392-94*
Winchester College Chapel

A detail from the Jesse window given by the founder to Winchester College; replaced by a copy in the early nineteenth century. Approximately a third of the original window has now been recovered, and is once more the property of the College, this detail being part of the original glass recovered. It is the work of 'Thomas Glazier', of Oxford, whose 'firm' was also responsible for the New College glass (part of the New College Jesse window is now in the South Choir aisle of York Minster). The glass illustrated was sold by Messrs. Betton & Evans who had been commissioned to restore it early in the nineteenth century, and who supplied in its place copies. The fact apparently was unnoticed for some years. They sold it for use in a mortuary chapel. This photograph, taken before the restoration work at present (1949) in progress on the glass had begun, gives some idea of the damage to the glass by corrosion.

PLATE 48   *Book of Hours and Psalter c. 1405*
British Museum, Royal MS. 2. A. XVIII

Executed after 1401, probably soon after; the artist appears to sign himself 'de Daer'. Our plate shows (*a*) the Annunciation; on either side are pictures of the owner of the manuscript and his wife (*b*) St. George fighting the dragon.

PLATES 49, 50   *Book of Hours 'of Elizabeth the Queene'. Fifteenth century.*
First Half
Now in the Library of C. W. Dyson Perrins, Esq.

Described by Dr. Eric Millar as the finest surviving English fifteenth-century Book of Hours. It contains the signature of Elizabeth of York, and this gives it its name. It was written apparently for Cecily Neville, wife of Henry Beauchamp, Duke of Warwick. Our plates show (49) the arrest in the Garden of Gethsemane (50) the Crucifixion. Pl. 49 is the size of the original. Pl. 50, which is in the original the same size as Pl. 49, has been enlarged in our reproduction to show details which would otherwise be lost in the process.

PLATE 51 (a) and (b)   *Wall Paintings. Between 1479 and 1488*
                                                        Eton College

This series of paintings in grisaille, with touches of colour (e.g. in the stained glass windows shown in the background of (*a*)) must have been a magnificent series. One of those who worked on the paintings was William Baker, and a suggestion has been made that this man was also the carver (named William Berkeley or Baker), who worked on the carved stalls for St. George's Chapel, Windsor, at this same date.

PLATES 52-56

These plates form an appendix, outside the main sequence, and references are given at the foot of each to that part of the book to which each relates. It may be desirable to give the whereabouts of the objects illustrated. The jewellery of Pls. 52 (*a*) and (*b*) is in the British Museum. For Pls. 52 (*c*) and (*d*) and Pl. 53 (*a*), see notes on p. 42 above. The original of Pl. 53 (*b*), the *Gospels of St. Augustine,* is in Corpus Christi College, Cambridge; of 53 (*c*) in the British Museum; of 53 (*d*), *Codex Aureus,* in Stockholm; of 54 (*b*) in Vienna; of 54 (*c*) and 55 (*a*), (*b*) and (*c*) in the British Museum; of 56 (*a*) in Winchester, 56 (*b*) and (*c*) in the Bodleian Library, Oxford.

I hope that it may eventually be possible to publish a documented discussion of the relationship between the Winchester Bible hand illustrated in 56 (*a*)—*The Master of the Apocrypha Drawings*—and that of the *Bodleian Terence* illustrated in 56 (*b*) and (*c*). The parallels extend far beyond the general similarity apparent at once. The extraordinary style of hairdressing on the main figure in 56 (*b*) is repeated again and again by this hand in the *Bible* and this hand alone, as is the remarkable serrated edge to the foot of a garment, the architectural feature like two ears, at the top of the turret, with the trident above it, and the dragging down of the eye in the drawing of the face. A full analysis would bring out some interesting points as to the methods of twelfth-century illumination.

Index

I. BOOKS

(References in italics are to Plate numbers)

II. PERSONS

INDEX

III. SUBJECTS REPRESENTED

INDEX

DECORATIVE FOLIO DECORATIVE FOLIO

('The Animal Folio')

Plate 9

From the Book of Durrow. Northumbrian, c. 670 A.D. See p. 42
See p. 42

(b)

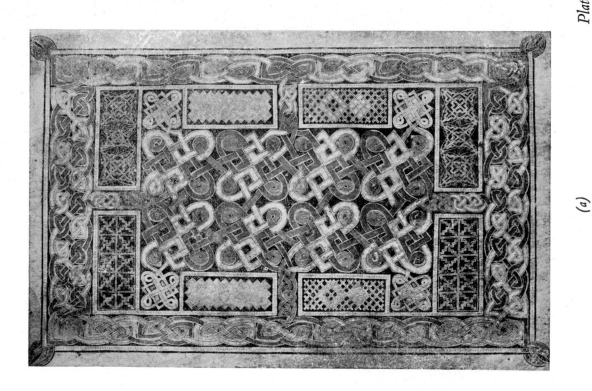

(a)

Plate 10

DECORATIVE FOLIOS

(That on the right damaged)

From the Book of Durrow, Northumbrian, c. 670 A.D. See p. 42

Plate 11

THE LION OF ST. MARK

From the Echternach Gospels. Northumbrian, c. 695 A.D. See p. 42

Plate 12

DETAIL FROM PLATE 13

Northumbrian Style, c. 710 A.D. Possibly executed in Wales. See p. 43

Plate 13

DECORATIVE FOLIO

(The 'Cruciform Folio')

From the so-called Gospels of St. Chad. Northumbrian Style, c. 710 A.D. Possibly executed in Wales. See p. 43

Plate 14

DECORATIVE FOLIO

('The Cruciform Folio')

From the Lindisfarne Gospels. Northumbrian, c. 710 A.D. See p. 43

(a) THE EVANGELIST ST. LUKE

(b) THE EVANGELIST ST. JOHN

Plate 15

From the Lindisfarne Gospels. Northumbrian, c. 710 A.D. See p. 43

SCS MARCUS .

Plate 16

THE EVANGELIST MARK

Possibly painted at York, c. 1000 A.D. See p. 44

Plate 17

THE EVANGELIST ST. LUKE WRITING

With his symbol of the Winged Bull

Detail enlarged from the Grimbald Gospels. New Minster, Winchester. c. 1020 A.D. See p. 44

Plate 18

THE THREE PERSONS OF THE TRINITY IN MEDALLIONS SUPPORTED BY FLYING ANGELS

Detail from the frontispiece to St. John's Gospel in the Grimbald Gospels. New Minster, Winchester, c. 1020 A.D. See p. 44

Plate 19

VIRGIN AND CHILD, IN A MEDALLION SUPPORTED BY ANGELS

From the Grimbald Gospels (detail from the opening page of St John's Gospel), New Minster, Winchester, c. 1020 A.D. See p. 44

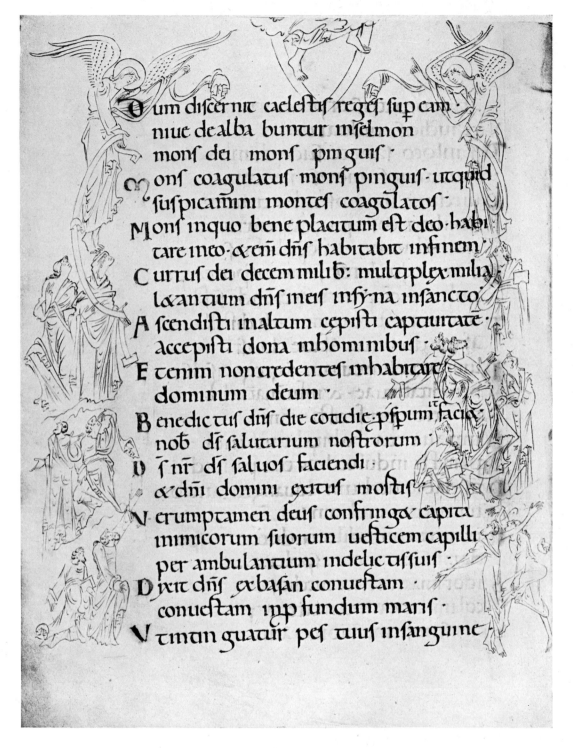

Plate 20

THE ASCENSION

At the top are the feet of the ascending Christ

Above, left and right, angels

Below, the Eleven, with the Virgin Mary

Illustrating *Psalm lxviii, v. 18*

Bury St. Edmunds, c. 1020 A.D. See p. 44

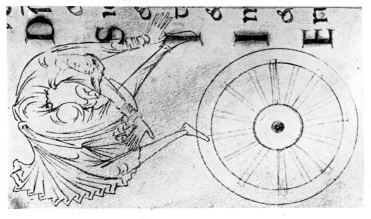

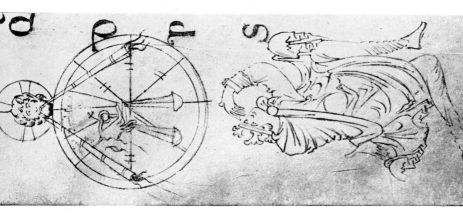

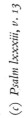

(c) *Psalm lxxxiii, v. 13*

(a) Souls carried to Abraham's bosom

(b) The Almighty, with a pair of
scales; (below) King David

Plate 21

THREE DETAILS FROM THE VATICAN PSALTER

Bury St. Edmunds, c. 1020 A.D. See p. 44

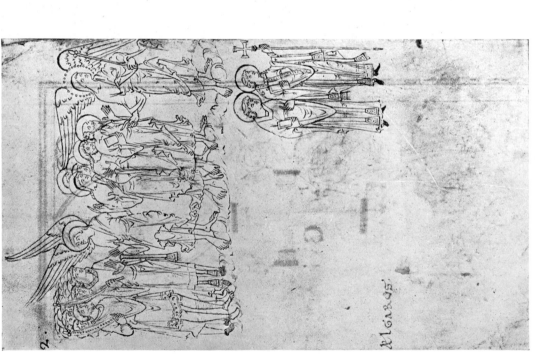

Plate 22

SAINTS, CONFESSORS, AND THE ABBOT OF THE NEW MINSTER
AWAITING ENTRY TO THE HEAVENLY CITY
THE CONTEST OF THE DEVIL AND ST. PETER FOR SOULS
THE DAMNED ENTERING THE MOUTH OF HELL

New Minster Winchester, about AD. 1030 (?)

Plate 23

ST. PAUL SHAKING THE VIPER INTO THE FIRE

Canterbury Cathedral (wall painting), c. 1160 A.D. *See p. 46*

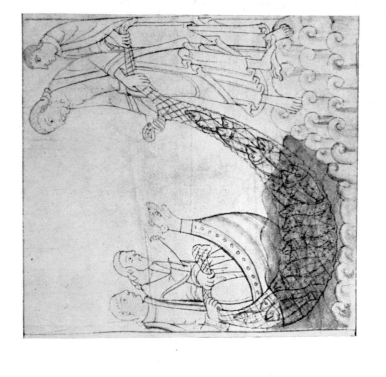

(a) THE ENTOMBMENT

(b) THE MIRACULOUS DRAUGHT OF FISHES

Plate 24

Bury St. Edmunds, c. 1100 A.D. *See p. 45*

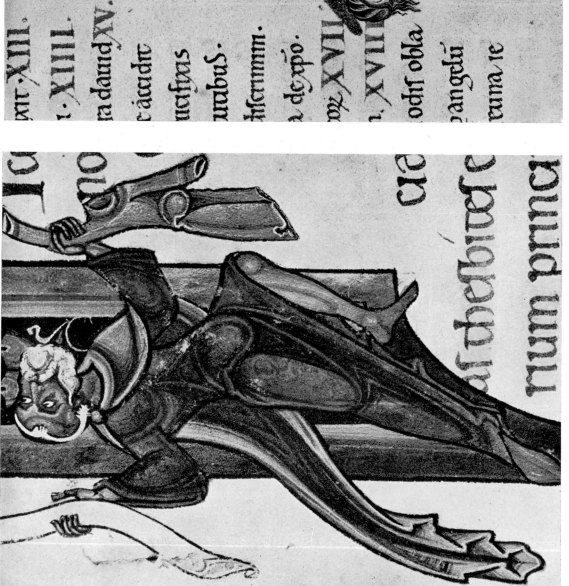

Plate 25

(a) ELISHA CATCHING THE CLOAK OF ELIJAH

(2 Kings ii, 13)

(b) THE YOUNG MAN SLAYS THE AMALEKITE

(2 Samuel i, 15)

From the Winchester Bible, Old Minster, Winchester, c. 1160 A.D.

Plate 26

TYPE AND ANTITYPE FROM THE OLD AND NEW TESTAMENTS

(Above) David rescuing a sheep from a bear, prefiguring Christ casting out a devil

(Below) David rescuing a lamb from the lion's jaws, prefiguring the harrowing of Hell

Old Minster, Winchester, c. 1175 A.D. See p. 46

Plate 27

THE BATTLE OF SAMARIA

(1 *Maccabees vii*; the arm and head are those of Nicanor, *v. 47*)

From the Winchester Bible. Old Minster, Winchester, c. 1160 A.D. See p. 46

Plate 28

THE DEATH IN BATTLE OF JUDAS MACCABEUS

THE ENTOMBMENT OF JUDAS MACCABEUS

From the Winchester Bible. Old Minster, Winchester, c. 1160 A.D. See p. 46

Plate 29

THE PARABLE OF THE SOWER

THE SEED FALLING BY THE WAYSIDE AND EATEN BY BIRDS

(The sower's head is apparently a modern restoration)

Canterbury Cathedral (glass), late XIIth Century, See p. 47

Plate 30

THE PATRIARCH JARED (*Luke iii, 13*)

(Here spelt IERETH)

Canterbury Cathedral (glass), late XIIth Century. See p. 47

Plate 31

(Above) CHRIST CRUCIFIED, BETWEEN TWO ROBBERS

(Below) THE WORD FROM THE CROSS TO THE VIRGIN AND ST. JOHN;
AND THE DEAD CHRIST

Detail enlarged from a Book of Hours. By W. de Brailes, c. 1240 A.D. See pp. 20, 47

Plate 32

THE SECOND ANGEL, WATCHED BY ST. JOHN,
SOUNDS HIS TRUMPET (*Revelation viii, 8*)

Enlarged detail from the Dyson Perrins Apocalypse. XIIIth Century, second half. See p. 47

Plate 33

THE SIXTH ANGEL, WATCHED BY ST. JOHN, POURING FROM
HIS PHIAL ON TO THE RIVER EUPHRATES *(Revelation xvi, 12)*

From the Dyson Perrins Apocalypse, XIIIth Century, second half. See p. 47

Plate 34

A SAINT (PROBABLY ST. JOHN)

From the Oscott Psalter. XIIIth Century, last quarter. See p. 48

Plate 35

MICHAEL FIGHTS AGAINST THE DRAGON (*Revelation xii, 7*)

XIVth Century, first quarter. See p. 48

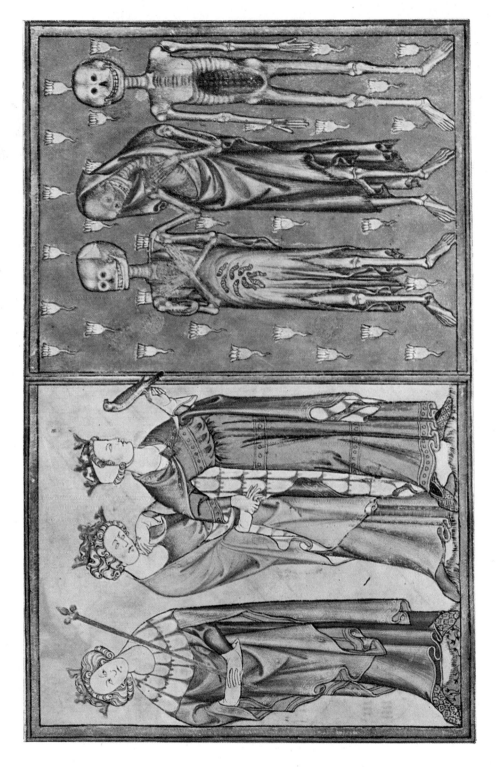

Plate 36

THE THREE LIVING AND THE THREE DEAD

Detail, approximately full-size, from the Psalter of Robert de Lisle. East Anglian XIVth Century, end of first quarter. See p. 48

Plate 37

THE HARROWING OF HELL

THE DEPOSITION

THE ENTOMBMENT

PILATE AND THE WATCH (*Matthew xxvii, 62-65*)

Considerably reduced, from the Psalter of Robert de Lisle. East Anglian XIVth Century, end of first quarter. See p. 48

Plate 38

VIRGIN AND CHILD

At the foot, a young lion and dragon (*Psalm xci, v. 13*)

Above, two angels censing

On either side, angels and saints (Catherine and Margaret)

Considerably reduced, from the Psalter of Robert de Lisle. East Anglian XIVth Century, end of first quarter. See p. 48

Plate 39

THE CRUCIFIED CHRIST, WITH THE VIRGIN AND ST. JOHN

The figure below the Cross is Adam

Above are the angels of the sun and moon, and the pelican in her piety

Considerably reduced, from the Psalter of Robert de Lisle. East Anglian XIVth Century, end of first quarter. See p. 48

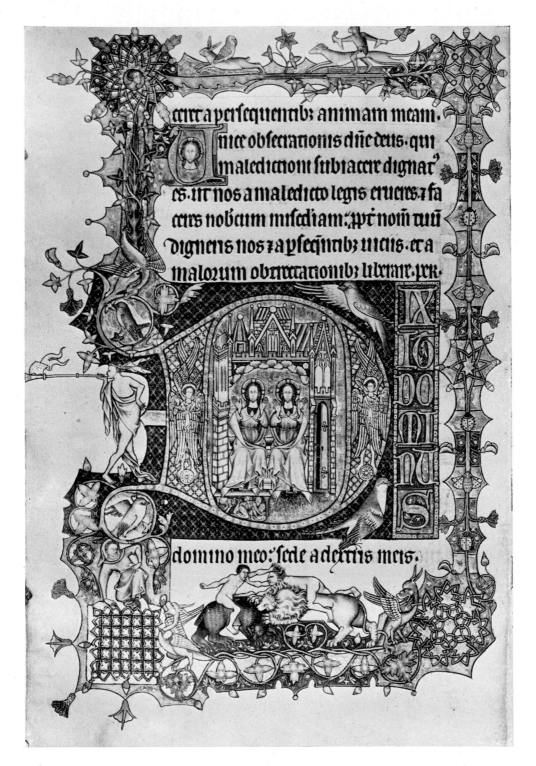

Plate 40

THE LORD SAID UNTO MY LORD, SIT THOU ON MY RIGHT HAND,
UNTIL I MAKE THINE ENEMIES THY FOOTSTOOL (*Psalm cx, v. 1*)

From the Ormesby Psalter. East Anglian, c. 1310. See p. 49

Plate 41

(Above) KILLING THE UNICORN

(Below) THE HERALD OF THE RENAISSANCE

Details from Plate 40, from the Ormesby Psalter. East Anglian, c. 1310. See p. 49

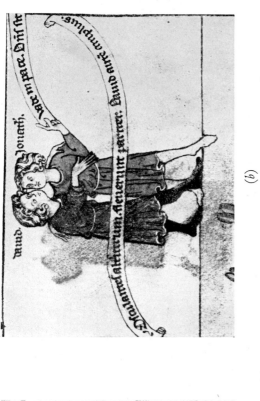

(a)

(b)

(c)

(d)

Plate 42

DRAWINGS FROM THE TICKHILL PSALTER

See p. 49

Plate 43

(Above) CHRIST TEACHING IN THE TEMPLE

(Below) THE VIRGIN PROTECTS A PILGRIM OVERTAKEN
BY THE TIDE

From the Queen Mary Psalter. XIVth Century, first quarter. *See p. 49*

(a) A SCENE FROM CREATION

(b) Above, THE QUARREL OF HAGAR AND SARAH

Below, HAGAR PUTS ISHMAEL UNDER THE SHRUB

THE ANGEL SHOWS HER THE WELL (*Genesis xxi, 17*)

Plate 44

From the Queen Mary Psalter, reduced. XIVth Century, first quarter. See p. 49

(a)

(b)

(c)

(d)

Plate 45

(a) THE HUNT

(b) and (c) AN OWL MOBBED

(d) LION AND GRIFFON

Details from the Queen Mary Psalter (approximately full-size). XIVth Century, first quarter. See p. 49

Plate 46

KING RICHARD II ADORES THE VIRGIN AND CHILD

The figures with the King are St Edmund, St Edward the Confessor, and John the Baptist

English, c. 1395. See p. 50

Plate 47

VIRGIN AND CHILD; THE CHILD HOLDING A BIRD

From the Jesse Window, given to Winchester College by the Founder. By Thomas Glazier of Oxford, 1393. See p. 50

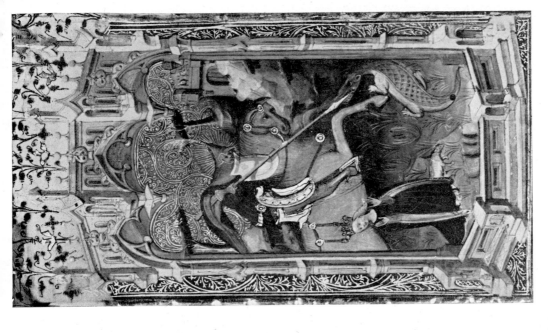

Plate 48   (b) ST. GEORGE SLAYS THE DRAGON

(a) THE ANNUNCIATION

Kneeling on either side are the owner of the book and his wife

Between 1401 and 1410. See p. 50

Plate 49

THE KISS OF JUDAS

Detail, considerably enlarged, from the Book of Hours 'of Elizabeth the Queene'. First half of XVth Century. See p. 50

Plate 50

THE CRUCIFIXION

(The soul of the robber on the right is being taken to Hell, the soul of the robber on the left to
Paradise. The kneeling figure is a confusion of the soldier and witness, *St. John xix, 34, 35*)

Detail, considerably enlarged, from the Book of Hours 'of Elizabeth the Queene'. First half of the XVth Century. See p. 50

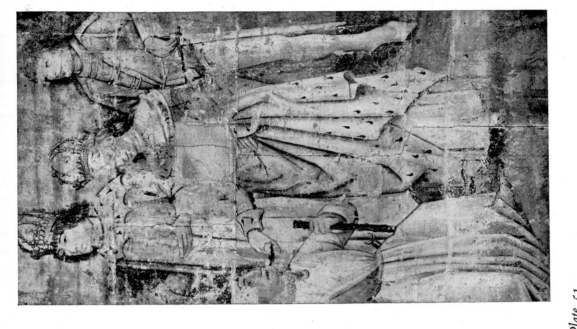

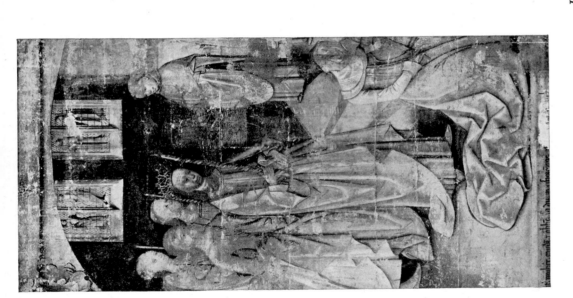

Plate 51

DETAILS FROM THE SERIES OF PAINTINGS REPRESENTING

THE MIRACLES OF THE VIRGIN

Eton College Chapel. Perhaps by William Baker, 1479-1488. See p. 51

(a)   (b)

BUCKLE AND CLASP

From Sutton Hoo Treasure (Anglo-Saxon, buried about 660 A.D.)

(c)   (d)

HEIFER-VITULUS—SYMBOL OF   SYMBOL OF ST. LUKE
ST. LUKE

Echternach Gospels, about 690 A.D.   *Book of Durrow, about 660 A.D.*

Plate 52

See Appendix I

(a)

SYMBOL OF ST. MATTHEW

Echternach Gospels, about 690 A.D.

(b)

ST. LUKE; WITH VIGNETTES OF
GOSPEL SCENES AND THE
SYMBOL OF ST. LUKE ABOVE

Gospels of St. Augustine

? Italian, about 550 A.D.

(c)

DAVID AND HIS MUSICIANS

Canterbury, VIIIth Century

(d)

ST. JOHN, WITH THE SYMBOL
OF ST. JOHN ABOVE

Canterbury, VIIIth Century

Plate 53

See Appendix I and Appendix II

(a)

(b)

PLATE 53 (b) REPEATED

for comparison of the Evangelist symbol, the winged bull, with that

of the Canterbury Gospels below

THE FOUR EVANGELISTS

Aachen, early IXth Century

(c)

DETAIL FROM THE INITIAL PAGE OF ST. LUKE'S GOSPEL

Canterbury Gospels, about 800 A.D.

Plate 54

See pp. 38-41

(a)

THE STORY OF SUSANNA AND THE ELDERS

(The Lothair Crystal)

French IXth Century

(b)

OCCUPATIONS OF THE MONTH: FEBRUARY,
THE PRUNING SEASON

Durham, about 1000 A.D

(c)

OCCUPATIONS OF THE MONTH: MARCH,
FELLING AND CARTING

Durham, about 1000 A.D.

Plate 55

See p. 15

(a)

THE PROPHET HOSEA

From the Winchester Bible, about 1150 A.D.

(b)

FIGURE IN CLASSICAL
COMIC ACTOR'S MASK

From the St. Albans Terence, about 1150 A.D.

(c)

SCENE FROM A COMEDY OF TERENCE

The actors are in classical masks

Probably St. Albans, about 1150 A.D.

Plate 56

See p. 19